To David Robl
one of Valley Forge's
Nonprofit Heroes!

Vaughn Town

2021

NONPROFIT HERO

NONPROFIT HERO

Five Easy Steps to
Successful Board Fundraising

Valerie M. Jones

ROWMAN & LITTLEFIELD

Lanham • Boulder • New York • London

Published by Rowman & Littlefield
An imprint of The Rowman & Littlefield Publishing Group, Inc.
4501 Forbes Boulevard, Suite 200, Lanham, Maryland 20706
www.rowman.com

Unit A, Whitacre Mews, 26-34 Stannary Street, London SE11 4AB

British Library Cataloguing in Publication Information Available

Library of Congress Cataloging-in-Publication Data

Names: Jones, Valerie M., 1957– author.
Title: Nonprofit hero : five easy steps to successful board fundraising / Valerie M. Jones.
Description: Lanham : Rowman & Littlefield, [2018] | Includes bibliographical references and index.
Identifiers: LCCN 2018013532 (print) | LCCN 2018014772 (ebook) | ISBN 9781538115039 (ebook) | ISBN 9781538115022 (cloth : alk. paper)
Subjects: LCSH: Fund raising. | Nonprofit organizations—Finance. | Boards of directors.
Classification: LCC HV41.2 (ebook) | LCC HV41.2 .J66 2018 (print) | DDC 658.15/224—dc23

LC record available at https://lccn.loc.gov/2018013532

♾️™ The paper used in this publication meets the minimum requirements of American National Standard for Information Sciences—Permanence of Paper for Printed Library Materials, ANSI/NISO Z39.48-1992.

Printed in the United States of America

To my three favorite authors: my mother, Annette Bousquet Jones; my husband, Don Lessem; and my son, Spencer Koelle; and to my daughter, Lucy Koelle, who is, true to her name, the light of my life. To John and Barbara Koelle, who took Spence and Lucy to Oz and 221 B Baker Street, and taught them to love stories.

CONTENTS

LIST OF FIGURES
AND TABLES

CHAPTER 1   UNLOCK THE SECRETS OF AUTHENTIC ASKING

CHAPTER 2   THE FIVE STEPS

ACKNOWLEDGMENTS

Authors are ingratiatingly modest when acknowledging the friends and colleagues who helped them develop their books. They write paeans of appreciation to a long list of people you don't know and couldn't care less about.

Not me.

There I was, happily running a successful consulting business. Then I took a course with a teacher to learn Sufi meditation and become a more spiritual person, not to change my career. When I said I wanted to create a new kind of fundraising, he called me on it. What could I do? I went home, developed it, and used it to train client boards. Eileen Cuniffe, director of the arts and business council's board training program, asked me to speak every year, providing a steady stream of victims . . . um, I mean accomplished students.

I was okay with that.

But my husband, Don Lessem, couldn't let well enough alone.

He thought I should write a book. Easy for him to say. He's authored more than fifty books, mostly about dinosaurs, and is famous if you're under twelve years old. He bugged me so relentlessly that I started writing. Then my friend Zofia Kostyrko jumped on the bandwagon. Zofia is a brilliant artist with a hearing problem. She's deaf to excuses. She paid me to write. (Please buy this book so I can pay her back.)

Then Liz Dow, CEO of LEADERSHIP Philadelphia, invited me to join her in taking a summer writing course. "Aw, bummer!" I said. "They're full up." Until they weren't. The day before class started, someone cancelled, I got a call, and Liz and I were off. We had a great professor, wonderful classmates. And, yes, I was back to writing this book.

But publishers want authors who are social media hotshots, right? Ha! I was barely on Facebook. Jasmine Kurtz, a brilliant young addition to my firm, developed a plan to rectify the situation. Interns Maran Collett and Kristen Lamb traitorously backed her up. By the end of the summer, Jasmine had become our firm's first social media manager and I had a cyber voice.

I should have known I was doomed when nonprofit marketing guru Gail Bower agreed to be my writing partner. She called every other Friday morning to check my progress and share her own. Faithfully. Consistently. Intelligently. Next summer's crop of interns made the situation even worse. Roman Shemakov developed a speaker's plan for this mythical tome while Emma Sniegowski crafted the book's marketing proposal. My dear friend Alex Knox, previously a magazine editor, now a D.C. acupuncturist (really!) gave the *Nonprofit Hero* book proposal a final polish. It wasn't my fault. *They* made it a crisp, relevant, and impressively well-researched book proposal.

Still, I looked forward to months of rejection before I had to produce anything.

Wrong again.

Editor Charles Harmon of Rowman & Littlefield expressed immediate interest. Like, within twelve hours. This guy is a respected professional who has published thousands of books. What was he thinking? Alarmed, I turned to my college classmate, literary agent Barbara Berson. She offered to represent me even though her firm, the Helen Heller Agency, doesn't handle nonfiction. I mean, if you can't trust someone who watched you do stupid things in college, who can you trust?

For the next three months, I wrote furiously. My firm's three young associates were mutinously supportive. Rachel Kilker updated the speaker's plan while Erin Busbee handled clients with such panache I had nowhere left to hide. In the final stretch, Karen Medina prepared the manuscript and illustrations for submission.

(Note to self: stop hiring smart young people.)

Of course, there were other conspirators. Editor Eliot Kaplan and his gorgeous wife, *Today Show*'s financial editor, Jean Chatsky, invited us back to their beach house despite my tendency to blather on about the book. I thought journalists delivered cutting repartee while glaring at you through a haze of cigarette smoke.

Apparently, I was misinformed.

I'm partly responsible for luring Barbara Silzle into the arts so I guess it's only fair that she, now executive director of the Philadelphia Cultural Fund, aided and abetted this book. I wish I could blame Eileen Heisman for something, but other than her inspiring leadership of the National Philanthropic Trust and an unshakable belief in human generosity, she has annoyingly few flaws.

Others helped, but they bribed me to leave their names off this list.

In my opinion, the best defense against becoming an author is to surround yourself with self-absorbed slackers who lack imagination. Tell no one of your intentions. Avoid friends and even your spouse. And for heaven's sake, don't hire bright young talent.

Those kids will get you published before you know what hit you.

PREFACE

If you serve on a nonprofit board, you probably hate doing the one thing upon which your cause depends: fundraising.

As it turns out, your instincts are right and most of what you think you know about fundraising is wrong. You should *not* ask your friends for money if you think they will turn you down or avoid you. You should *not* ask strangers or solicit friends who know nothing about your cause. Nor should you ask for a gift if you don't know who to ask, how much to request, or what to pitch.

Nonprofit Hero will show you a better way. In it, you'll learn to fundraise authentically and in ways at which you'll excel. It starts with the easiest step, thanking, and proceeds until, by the time you get to asking, you're practically guaranteed a gift.

As a professional fundraiser, I ask in ways that play to my strengths and work around my weaknesses, luxuries rarely afforded to volunteers. You, poor soul, get wheedled with entreaties or bludgeoned with ultimatums. "Please submit the names and emails of twenty of your friends," or, "Everyone must sell ten gala tickets," or, "Raise $5,000 by next month." The unspoken subtext being that if you don't, you're off the board.

Without a clue as to who or how to ask, you freeze. Naturally.

I'm here to lubricate your asking joints, to show you that you have a heart, a brain, and courage when it comes to fundraising.

If you're the reluctant volunteer fundraiser for whom this book is written, you're not alone. According to BoardSource, 65 percent of nonprofit chairmen give their own boards a grade of C, D, or F in fundraising.

I've worked with thousands of smart, accomplished, articulate, and dedicated board members. Invariably, fundraising is their least favorite task.

Even if you're an experienced nonprofit executive or development director, *Nonprofit Hero* can ramp up your asking skills and invigorate your philanthropic leadership. *Nonprofit Hero* contains training activities to enliven meetings and build board expertise. It's eminently sensible, listing thirty things your board can do, right now, for free, to help you raise money.

Nonprofit Hero is a quick, light read, full of bite-sized tips and memorable stories. You can go through it from start to finish or skip around, discovering your asking personality one day and where to find prospects the next. You can develop a compelling case for support or familiarize yourself with grantmaker lingo. *Nonprofit Hero* is the kind of book you can skim five minutes before you walk into a board meeting and sound . . . well, sound like a hero.

Chapter 1 goes right to the heart of the matter, helping you identify and address your fundraising fears. You'll learn to develop a personal mission statement and align it with that of your nonprofit. I even give you permission to leave a bad board for a better one, if that's what you need to do. You'll learn where the money comes from, where it goes, and how fundraising works. You'll discover a kinder, gentler way of asking that builds on your unique approach to the world.

Chapter 2 explains the five steps of fundraising, illustrated with real-life stories drawn from my own experience. Each case study makes a point, emphasizes a positive attribute, and provides handy pointers you can use right away. The five-step method ensures you always know where you are in the fundraising process and what to do next.

Chapter 3 describes the sixteen asking personalities that I've created. Consult the quick tips chart to learn who, how, and where you should ask, as well as which of the five steps you'll favor. The chart is followed by your in-depth asking profile, and that of fifteen other personality types. Your profile explains how *you* can best thank, engage, research, cultivate, and ask; your asking strengths, possible weaknesses, and what others can do to help you succeed.

Chapter 4 shows you how to prepare your pitch, your mind, and even your body before asking. You'll learn how to navigate a yes, no, or maybe, either on your own or with an asking partner. You'll find guidance on leading a development committee, on development plans, database needs, and proper staff/board etiquette. I'll review the fundamentals of corporate, foundation, and government grantmaking. By the end of this chapter, you'll be ready to get your cape on.

Samples and templates save precious time and effort. Why should you reinvent the wheel? The Fundraiser's Toolkit contains resources described throughout this book, as well as a handy directory of online resources, should you wish to learn more.

Fundraising books are usually written for professionals, not for board members. Those designed for volunteers can be overly technical, telling you more than you need to know and leaving you none the wiser, or giving you sound advice without a framework for implementation, so you're not sure how the pieces fit together.

Nonprofit Hero is one of the few fundraising books written exclusively for board members, and the *only* one that shows each reader how to ask in the way that's right for *them*. This book is your personal fundraising coach, a friendly, funny, empathetic, experienced, and wise coach, standing right by your side, whose sole concern is your success. I know the *Nonprofit Hero* method works because I've proved it.

Controlled, anonymous pre- and post-training surveys found that 100 percent of the *Nonprofit Hero*–trained boards realized there was something they *could* do to help fundraise and 100 percent declared that they *would*. The number of potential donors they could identify doubled, and the rapidity with which they planned to contact donors increased 80 percent. After the training, 92 percent could see themselves soliciting gifts of $1,000 or more, whereas only two-thirds were willing to do so before the training. Half could see themselves giving more to their own nonprofits.

Board development chair Wil Woldenberg, president of Entegrit, wrote that by using my principles, he "doubled our donor base in six months!" An Arts and Business Council alumnus reported, "Val's is the best training I've ever had, of any kind, ever!" A veteran NPR grantswriter reported, "I've attended numerous trainings on 'making the ask.' Yours was hands-down the best." A Dress for Success board member summed it up by saying, "Every volunteer board member should take Val's training."

Nonprofit Hero is the distillation of every course I've taught, every article I've read, every board I've coached, and everyone I've mentored. It works. And now it's yours.

That said, *Nonprofit Hero* may be the first fundraising book with Sufi roots.

Five years ago, I studied Sufi meditation with my teacher. The first semester we focused on health, the second on relationships, and the third on our careers. He asked how we felt about our work and what we hoped to do in the future. Some of my classmates felt trapped, some enjoyed their work, many were unsure of what to do next. I shared my passion for fundraising, the pleasure it gave me, and satisfaction I took in the positive impact I'd made.

"So, what do you want?" My teacher asked.

"I just want everyone to fundraise the Val way," I answered.

I explained that most people dread fundraising, and that it makes board members feel inadequate. They get squirmy at the very mention of the "F" word. I explained that two clients had, independently, looked at me oddly and asked, "Are you a Buddhist fundraiser?" They were delighted with the money we'd raised, but they found my approach so different, so gentle, that they weren't sure what to think.

I told my teacher that I wanted boards to realize that everyone can participate in the *process*. To discover that they don't have to be extraverts to fundraise. That they should ask in their own unique way. I told him we needed them. That they're my heroes.

"What are you going to do about it?" he asked.

"I guess I'll invent a new way to train people."

The following Monday, I got started.

I covered my office walls with flip charts. At the top of each sheet, I wrote a phrase I used with my clients: "Nothing sells the zoo like the zoo," or "Everyone can thank." If I said it repeatedly, I reasoned, it must be central to my philosophy. I added pictures. I added quotes. I listed experiences that illustrated each point I hoped to make. I gave it a framework. I added sheets. I took them off. I winnowed it down to its essence.

Around this time, one of Philadelphia's most brilliant and selfless citizens, Liz Dow, invited me to address a group of nonprofit leaders. I accepted. Now I had a deadline.

I debuted my method before the LEADERSHIP Philadelphia Collaborative in September of 2012. Two months later, during the last weekend of my yearlong meditation course, I invited my classmates to attend an after-dinner presentation. As they listened, they were delighted, seeing the lessons we'd learned together woven through my methodology.

For the next four years, my training evolved. I created a three-hour format for board retreats and a short version for conferences. I devised sixteen in-depth asking profiles. I gave talks and led board retreats every chance I got. I turned down other assignments to focus on this work. I've trained more than a thousand board members and development professionals. I expect to train thousands more in the years ahead.

After they learn the *Nonprofit Hero* method, participants report one overwhelming feeling: relief. They're *relieved* that they won't be rejected or alienate their friends, that they don't have to embarrass themselves or let down their cause.

After you've read *Nonprofit Hero*, you, like them, will know how to cast yourself as a star, and how to turn your fears into strengths. You'll be able to leverage your asking personality. You'll stride through the five steps of fundraising, making your case sincerely and with compelling confidence. You'll help donors achieve their heart's desire.

You'll become your very own kind of nonprofit hero.

❶

UNLOCK THE SECRETS OF AUTHENTIC ASKING

"The cave you fear to enter holds the treasure you seek."

—Joseph Campbell

HONOR YOUR FEARS

If you've ever applied to college or for a job, asked for a raise, a date, a gift or even to change seats on a plane, you may have experienced the fear of asking. Your unease starts before you open your mouth. It builds as you fumble for the right words. You imagine a thousand reasons why they'll say no. Finally, you ask, whispering it inaudibly, putting it badly, or blurting it out in a rush. The moment after you've spoken, your anxiety peaks.

As your appeal hangs in the air, milliseconds seem like months. You're suspended in that dreadful silence after you've asked, but before they answer. Your fate, it seems, is in their hands. This apprehension can be very painful. You may backpedal, withdrawing your request before the person you're asking even has a chance to consider it. "But this is probably a bad time," you say, or, "I know it's too much," or, "Please don't feel you have to."

No wonder we hate asking.

Asking is vital to our lives, but anathema to our culture.

Americans value self-reliant pioneers and rugged individualists. Hundreds of ESPN documentaries recount stories of athletes who overcome incredible odds . . . alone. A daring secret agent takes on the military, a corporate conglomerate, or, preferably, the entire world . . . singlehandedly. Sure, they may pick up a lover or sidekick along the way, but it's the self-sufficient champion whom we idolize. The name of *Star Wars'* roguish hero says it all. Han *Solo.*

We want to hire "self-starters" because *real* Americans blaze their own paths, right?

Maybe they do in the movies, but not in real life. We ask and ask and ask, and others ask us in turn. Every day. Those who ask well, who know who, how, and when to ask, succeed. For themselves, their families, their employers, and their causes. They ask with integrity and strategically. They rarely hear "no," but when they do, they are unfazed, even cheerful, remaining on good terms with those who have declined their requests.

We ask all the time, either badly or well. Sadly, some of us don't ask at all.

If, in our heart of hearts, we believe the answer will be "no," why bother? Too often, we don't. Then we spend hours, days, or even a lifetime wondering what might have been.

We justify our lack of initiative. We blame ourselves or others. We regret the path not taken. We come to fear asking so much, we may even blind ourselves to opportunity, learning not to see it at all. Just to avoid asking.

I ask for a living, and I love it. I'm a fundraiser. I've raised more than $175 million, not from the mega-rich but from organizations you've never heard of and from many, many generous people like you. Their gifts have helped to build a veterinary hospital. They've mounted new plays and fed and educated children. Their contributions have helped protect the remains of a saber-toothed tiger and one of Leonardo da Vinci's notebooks. How did this happen? Someone reached out. Someone took a risk. Someone asked for support.

I didn't write this book for my colleagues in development (another word for fundraising). I wrote it for my nonprofit heroes, the valiant souls who volunteer their time and give their money as well.

There are more than 20 million nonprofit board members in the United States alone. Most hate to do the one thing upon which their charity depends: fundraising. If you're one of them, this book is for you.

And you're not alone.

BoardSource, global experts in nonprofit board leadership, found that although board members themselves are generous, more than half (60 percent) say they're uncomfortable asking others to contribute. In response to a recent survey, 65 percent of nonprofit board chairs and CEOs awarded their own boards a grade of C, D, or F in fundraising.

A client once confessed that the idea of "dunning his friends" appalled him. If you're like him, you'd rather donate your own time and money than ask someone else to give, even though you know how desperately your library, theater, or homeless shelter needs the money. If you're like my client, you'll do almost *anything* for your nonprofit—except fundraise.

Clearly, fundraising has an image problem.

Let's try a little free association. What pops up when you read this word? Fundraising.

At best, it conjures up words such as *responsibility, committee, Girl Scout Cookies*, or *tithe*. More likely, *begging, annoying, phone calls during dinner*, or *junk mail* come to mind.

But what if there was a better way to ask? What if the process of getting gifts called forth the best in you, the part that's empathetic, creative, honorable, observant, connected, curious, vibrant, responsive, generous, confident, inspired, attentive, good humored, prepared, noble, and transformative?

What if there was a way you could become an asking superhero?

There is.

I've taught hundreds of people to fundraise. Using my method, they ask clearly and authentically. They participate in the asking process in ways they find comfortable and effective. They do well right from the start, getting better and gaining confidence as they go. Sometimes they look back, elated and a bit surprised, to find they've raised thousands, even millions of dollars.

They use the five-step method I'll share with you.

As a nonprofit hero, you'll turn fundraising upside down. You'll begin with easy steps like thanking and build momentum so that by the time you get to asking, you've already succeeded. Most important, I will help you become the *person* who gets a gift. For no matter how good your technique, how compelling your reasoning, or how passionate your heart, if the wrong "you" shows up—the "you" who feels worthless, incompetent, or overly demanding—then you'll be the person who gets the "no."

Let's leave that person behind.

I invite you to get used to the thrill of "yes."

ACTIVITIES

This book contains a series of activities. Most take just a few minutes to complete. Skip these activities and you'll still learn a lot. *Do* the activities and you'll be *given* a lot.

ACTIVITY: Giving Dos & Don'ts

One of the best ways to understand giving is to put yourself in your donor's position, to reflect on your own experiences. Think of a contribution that you felt good about. Then recall a donation you wish you hadn't made, one that left a bad taste in your mouth. Jot down *why* these gifts gladdened your heart or dampened your spirits. If you're stumped for charitable examples, think of birthday, holiday, or wedding gifts you've given. The principles are the same.

Do: Gift that made me feel glad, satisfied, happy.

Gift: _____

Why? _____

_____

_____

_____

Don't: Gift I regretted.

Gift: _____

Why? _____

_____

_____

_____

Nonprofit heroes solicit gifts that are as much fun to give as they are to receive. Imagine yourself in your donor's position and resolve to ask in ways that will make them happy. If you're struggling with this activity, you'll find examples in the Fundraiser's Toolkit section of this book.

TRUST YOUR INSTINCTS

Why aren't you asking? Americans give away *hundreds of billions of dollars* every year. So why doesn't your cause have all the money it needs?

As a fundraising consultant, I frequently ask nonprofit executives, "What's your biggest challenge and how can I help?" Interestingly, even those who need money badly are convinced that if enough people and organizations were properly asked, their cause would be well funded.

So, what's the problem? College presidents and soup kitchen directors alike complain of the board members who won't, don't, or can't ask for gifts.

You may be one of those non-fundraising board members. Yet you're one of your community's most accomplished, articulate, respected, and selfless leaders. You give generously and care deeply about your nonprofit's mission.

So why, when asked to solicit your friend for a gift, do you shrivel up and wish you were elsewhere? Why is fundraising at the bottom of your to-do list? Why, when you finally ask, do you feel awkward and insecure?

You shy away for powerful reasons.

I call them your *"Yeah, buts . . ."* As in, *"Yeah,* I'd like to ask for a major gift, *but . . ."*

I have good news for you. I *don't* want you to stifle or ignore your objections. I want you to *listen* to them. Honor them. And don't proceed until your *"Yeah, buts . . ."* are addressed. You have good instincts and following them is part of becoming a nonprofit hero. As you learn my method, your *"Yeah, buts . . ."* will diminish or cease to arise at all.

ACTIVITY: "Yeah, But . . ."

1. Think of someone you could ask to contribute $1,000 to your nonprofit.
2. Get out your cell phone and look up their number. Hit dial. When they answer, ask them.
3. Stop. Relax. Don't make that call.
4. Look inside yourself. How did you feel? Were you ready to ask? Probably not. What was your first hesitation? If you're like most of my clients, you thought, "Yeah, I want someone to give my nonprofit $1,000 but . . ."
5. Write down your *"Yeah, buts . . ."* All of them.

_____

_____

_____

_____

_____

_____

Hold on to this list. We'll revisit it later so that I can show you how to turn these fears and hesitations into your prescription for asking success. Turn to the Toolkit section of this book for a list of some of the most frequently experienced fundraising "Yeah, buts . . ."

HARNESS YOUR PASSION

> "Go confidently in the directions of your dreams. Live the life you have imagined."
>
> —Henry David Thoreau

A mission statement declares a company's, nonprofit's, or individual's aspirational purpose, their reason for being. Nonprofits post their mission statements on their websites, tout them in annual reports, print them on business cards, and include them in emails. Nonprofit mission statements strive to be exquisitely succinct. The Philadelphia Zoo is a $50-million-a-year organization with a wide array of programs and services. Here's their mission statement: "By connecting people with wildlife, the Philadelphia Zoo creates joyful discovery and inspires action for animals and habitats."

According to David LaPiana, author of *The Nonprofit Strategy Revolution*, the best mission statements don't just say what they do, such as, "Our mission is to provide services to Head Start kids." They say how the world will be different as a result: "Our mission is to ensure every child in our district starts school prepared to learn at grade level."

What about *your* mission statement?

Stephen Covey, author of *The Seven Habits of Highly Effective People*, was a big believer in personal mission statements, and so am I. These can be as short as a few lines or several pages long. To create your own, use the Covey Franklin mission statement builder, which is available online with free registration at http://msb.franklincovey.com.

The Covey/Franklin template encourages you to reflect on categories like performance: When am I at my best? When am I at my worst? And passion: What do I love doing at work? At home?

Developing your mission statement will prompt you to reflect on your natural talents, to imagine what you'd do if you weren't afraid to fail; if you had unlimited time and money. It asks you to consider what you'd want people to say of you at the end of your life, of your character and the difference you've made. It reminds you of things left undone that you could still do. It asks you to list the people who've influenced you the most and why. It invites you to consider your work/home balance (or lack thereof).

Though you'll need some quiet time to write your personal mission statement, it's helpful for many reasons, including fundraising. Once you articulate what you care about and hope to accomplish with your life, you'll know how your nonprofit's mission aligns with your own. You'll know why you're asking for money, and your requests will resonate with deeply personal authenticity.

For example, Annette, who sat on the board of a science museum, felt tongue-tied when inviting her friends to buy gala tickets or make gifts. Her personal mission statement revealed a strong affinity for education. This thread wasn't obvious to me or to her. Annette was a high-ranking human resources executive. She'd never been trained as an educator, but she loved to coach. As I got to know her better, I discovered that she succeeded professionally because she was so good at *teaching* employees to understand their benefits and to use them wisely.

Around this time, one of our educational funders withdrew. We had three months to replace the funds. Annette was dismayed. I offered to support her, and she sprang into action. We identified donors with a track record of supporting education. When she spoke to these donors, all of whom shared her passion, she was eloquent, persuasive, and persistent. Thanks in large part to Annette, we succeeded in raising the needed funds. The chairman of the board excused Annette from selling gala tickets because she was so much happier and more effective funding specific science education programs.

You must be willing, as Gandhi says, to "be the change you wish to see in the world." But what kind of change do you envision, precisely? Do you see a world where all pets are wanted pets? A world of full and honorable employment? Where there's universal access to clean drinking water? A cancer-free world?

Imagine you can make a better world just by asking for it. That you can do it confidently, in ways you'll be comfortable with, that honor your relationships and play to your strengths.

Because you can.

What if you write your mission statement and develop a vision for the future, only to discover you aren't in sync with the nonprofit you serve? Perhaps a friend asked you to join the board and it seemed like a good idea at the time, but it never quite clicked at a gut level. If you find yourself in this situation, you have my blessing to leave. Go find a nonprofit that excites you, makes you light up, and brings you closer to your heart's desire. There are thousands that need you. Find the right match, and your fundraising may mysteriously improve.

There are volunteer opportunities all around you. The Bridgespan Group (www.bridgespan.org) posts nonprofit board openings across the country, as does BoardNet (www.boardnetusa.org). Volunteer Match (www.volunteermatch.org) allows you to search for opportunities near you. There are nonprofit leadership chapters across the United States that provide board training and placement. Many are affiliated with your local chamber of commerce, but some are independent nonprofits, such as www.leadership philadelphia.org.

You may want to volunteer on a committee first, getting to know a nonprofit that interests you before you commit yourself to board service.

ACTIVITY: Personal Statement

Write your personal mission statement using http://msb.franklincovey.com.

You can find sample mission statements on the Greatness Wall of the Franklin Covey mission building community (http://msb.franklincovey.com/inspired/wall).

ENSURE YOU'RE WELL CAST

"The world is a stage, but the play is badly cast."

—Oscar Wilde

The perfect actor to play Pseudolus in *A Funny Thing Happened on the Way to the Forum* may not be cast as Willy Loman in *Death of a Salesman*. Sure, there are human chameleons like Meryl Streep who can become almost anyone. But they are the exceptions. Their ability to transform themselves is a craft they've perfected over decades.

The rest of us do best when we play to our strengths and work around our weaknesses. Fortunately, humans embody a glorious range of strengths, talents, and abilities. If you are reading this, you want to use your gifts to serve a cause you believe in.

I don't know if Albert Einstein could balance his checkbook, but if he couldn't, who cares? He changed our understanding of the universe by playing to his strengths. I'm no Einstein, but I'm very good at fundraising. My weaknesses include overcommitting and procrastination. I've developed strategies to compensate for these weaknesses, such as hiring staff to say no on my behalf. I meditate to turn scary projects into manageable ones. I delegate as much and as soon as possible. Most of my clients don't know about my weaknesses, and those that do, don't care . . . if I help them raise millions of dollars.

Like me, you probably prefer doing tasks at which you excel, avoiding the stuff you don't like or aren't good at.

Too often, all board members are assigned the same task. The chairperson may declare, "Everyone has to get a table sponsored." This one-size-fits-all approach means most board members are uncomfortable asking. They may sponsor the table themselves, feeling inadequate because they've failed to attract new supporters. Some boards depend on the few members who *are* good at fundraising. These champion askers often do more than their share, burn out, and quit the board. This lose-lose-lose situation frustrates staff and squanders board talent. It leaves nonprofits chronically underfunded and searching for "better" board members.

Wouldn't it be preferable if everyone played *a part* in the fundraising *process?* If we were all well cast, assigned roles we loved, and given tasks we're good at? Playing to your strengths is a crucial strategy for becoming a nonprofit hero.

To cast yourself so that you'll shine, it's helpful to know your strengths and weaknesses, talents and preferences. There are instruments designed to help you do so. Of necessity, they simplify human complexity and are descriptive, not predictive. One such tool is the Myers-Briggs Type Indicator (MBTI) test. Though commonly used in work and school settings, the MBTI was not developed by trained psychiatrists. In this context, think of it as a useful shorthand for the kinds of people you interact with every day. The MBTI describes sixteen personality types on four continuums: (1) Extraversion/Introversion, (2) Sensing/iNtuitive, (3) Thinking/Feeling, and (4) Judging/Perceiving.

Personality models such as the MBTI and Big Five have been around for decades. Their predictive ability has been both criticized and defended by practitioners and psychologists. I am using them for their *descriptive* ability. I have observed that certain kinds of people are more successful when they approach fundraising in certain ways. MBTI abbreviations serve as useful handles for tailoring the fundraising process to different kinds of individuals.

Some Myers-Briggs terms differ from the way these words are used in everyday language. Here's how the Myers & Briggs Foundation defines its four continuums, and the situations in which they apply.

- Favorite world: Do you prefer to focus on the outer world (Extraversion) or on your own inner world (Introversion)? This reflects where you prefer to put your attention and where you get your energy.
- Information: Do you prefer to focus on the basic information you take in (Sensing) or do you prefer to interpret and add meaning (iNtuitive)? A Sensing person tends to utilize his five senses to obtain information; while an iNtuitive person entertains input from internal thinking processes.
- Decisions: When making decisions, do you prefer to look first at the logic and consistency (Thinking) or first look at the people and special circumstances (Feeling)?
- Structure: In dealing with the outside world, do you prefer to get things decided (Judging) or do you prefer to stay open to new information and options (Perceiving)? Judging personalities prefer sequential, step-by-step mental processing, while Perceiving people prefer to react in a spontaneous and flexible manner.

Myers-Briggs types are abbreviated in a four-letter sequence, as follows:

- 1st letter: E (Extraversion) or I (Introversion)
- 2nd letter: S (Sensing) or N (iNtuitive)
- 3rd letter: T (Thinking) or F (Feeling)
- 4th letter: J (Judging) or P (Perceiving)

For example, a person leading with Introversion, iNtuitive, Feeling, and Perceiving preferences would be an INFP. There are MBTI distinctions we won't go into here, such as which of the four is your dominant function and the strength of your preferences on each of the four pairings. You may score as extreme in Feeling, or have only a mild preference, hovering near the Thinking/Feeling boundary.

I am neither a degreed psychiatrist nor a certified MBTI assessor. I am, however, a seasoned fundraiser who has trained more than a thousand individuals. I'll walk you through your best approach to each of the five steps of asking, based on your Myers–Briggs personality profile, and, based on your strengths, I'll note the steps where you'll absolutely shine.

A string of letters is not very evocative, so I've used nicknames to capture the essence of each profile. I've borrowed some of these and invented others. Whether you're an Artist, Protector, Counselor, Idealist, Good Steward, Strategist, Philosopher, Craftsman, Giver, Catalyst, Performer, Provider, Executive, Entrepreneur, Guardian, or Visionary, read on to discover your personal prescription for fundraising success.

No MBTI type is better than another, any more than it's better to be right- or left-handed. Some are more common than others. Table 1.1 presents the estimated percentage of each type in the U.S. population.

Table 1.1. Myers–Briggs frequency chart

MBTI as a Percentage of the Population			
ISTJ 11.6%	ISFJ 13.8%	INFJ 1.5%	INTJ 2.1%
ISTP 5.4%	ISFP 8.8%	INFP 4.4%	INTP 3.3%
ESTP 4.3%	ESFP 8.5%	ENFP 8.1%	ENTP 3.2%
ESTJ 8.7%	ESFJ 12.3%	ENFJ 2.5%	ENTJ 1.8%

Note: The Myers & Briggs Foundation. http://www.myersbriggs.org/my-mbti-personality-type/my-mbti-re sults/how-frequent-is-my-type.htm. The estimated frequency table was compiled from a variety of MBTI® results from 1972 through 2002, including data banks at the Center for Applications of Psychological Type; CPP, Inc; and Stanford Research Institute (SRI).

Notice that I counted 50.9% of our society. In Susan Cain's book *Quiet: The Power of Introverts in a World That Can't Stop Talking,* she points out that many introverts perform exceptionally and make great leaders, including Abraham Lincoln, Mahatma Gandhi, Rosa Parks, and Albert Einstein. Use the activity that follows to find your personality type, and keep it in mind as you read on.

It'll be fascinating, because it's all about you.

ACTIVITY: Find Your Asking Personality

Start by taking the Myers–Briggs Type Indicator (MBTI) test. Once you have your MBTI personality results, you can use it to find your asking personality in chapter 3.

You will get the most accurate results by having the Myers-Briggs Type Indicator personality test administered by a certified specialist. Perhaps you've already learned your type at school or work. If not, you can take the Myers–Briggs Type Indicator test online at www.mbtionline.com ($49). There are free knockoffs of the test, based on the same principles, but not approved by the Myers & Briggs Foundation. Here are two that may be close enough for our purpose.

www.humanmetrics.com/cgi-win/jtypes2.asp
www.16personalities.com/free-personality-test

Now record your type below:

Extraversion/Introversion (E or I)   _____
Sensing/iNtuitive (S or N)   _____
Thinking/Feeling (T or F)   _____
Judging/Perceiving (J or P)   _____
My MBTI type is: _____

Example: An Extraverted, iNtuitive, Thinking, and Judging person would be an ENTJ.

Once you know your MBTI type, go to chapter 3, "Do It Your Way," to discover your asking personality, and learn the best way for you to thank, engage, research, cultivate, and ask.

If you're borderline, such as ENTJ/ENFJ, you'll find useful tips in both profiles. If you disagree, read all the type descriptions and pick the one that feels like the best fit.

After all, you're the ultimate expert on you.

TURN FUNDRAISING UPSIDE DOWN

"Start by doing what's necessary, then do what's possible; and suddenly you are doing the impossible."

—St. Francis of Assisi

Where Charitable Giving Comes From: $410.02 billion

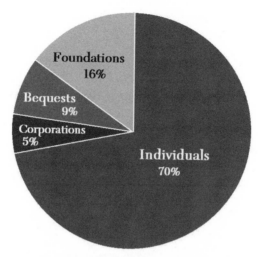

Fig. 1.1.   Where does the money come from?
Source: Giving USA 2018 Report: The Annual Report of Philanthropy for the Year 2017. www.GivingUSA.org

Who Gives the Money?

Forty years ago, Americans gave $25 billion a year to charities. At last report, they donate more than $410 billion annually. Even accounting for inflation, that's a dramatic increase. Through boom times and bad, this overall upward trend persists. Take a look at figure 1.1 to learn where these gifts come from. It may surprise you.

Many of us assume corporations make the biggest donations to charities. In fact, corporations provide only about 5 percent of charitable giving.

And what about foundations—the big establishments giving away millions and millions of dollars? Yes, they're responsible for 16 percent of that $410 billion, but most foundations are created by wealthy *individuals*. The Gates Foundation was formed by Bill and Melinda Gates, not by Microsoft. The same is true for many eponymous foundations; Mr. Mellon, Mr. Carnegie, and the Fords created the foundations that bear their names.

Most foundations are quite small. Ninety percent give away less than $1 million, and 65 percent donate less than $100,000 a year. Smaller foundations are often run by, and reflect the interests, beliefs, and values, of the *individuals* and families that endow them.

Gifts and bequests from *individuals* make up 70 percent of all giving in America. You and I, it turns out, are the source of most of that $410 billion a year. We are the big donors.

Who Gets the Money?

Who are the lucky recipients of all these gifts? As you can see in figure 1.2, we contribute to the nonprofits that are closest to our hearts and entwined in our lives. And we give because someone asked us.

Almost a third of our giving (31 percent) goes to religious organizations, to the churches, temples, or mosques where we worship. Next, we donate to education (14 percent), to our own schools and those of our children. Twelve percent of our gifts go to human services charities, because most of us feel we must help feed, clothe, and shelter the less fortunate members of our society.

Where Charitable Gifts Go:

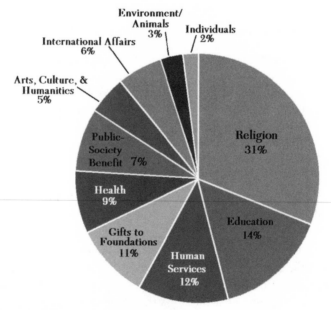

Fig. 1.2. Where does the money go?
Sources: Giving USA 2018 Report: The Annual Report of Philanthropy for the Year 2017. www.GivingUSA.org

Another 11 percent of our philanthropic dollars go to foundations, many of which are endowed in perpetuity. We give 9 percent of our largesse to health care (no surprise if one of your loved ones has suffered from cancer, Alzheimer's, or heart disease).

Gifts to these five categories—religion, education, human services, foundations, and health care—make up the lion's share (77 percent) of all private giving in the United States.

We distribute the rest of our gifts to nonprofits that benefit public society (7 percent), arts, culture, and the humanities (5 percent), international affairs (6 percent), animal/environmental causes (3 percent), and individuals (2 percent).

How Fundraising *Should* Work

The five steps in figure 1.3 reflect how fundraising is supposed to work. First, you identify prospective donors through *research*. There are lots of ways of doing this. They're in the news, they come to an event, or they have a family member suffering from a disease you hope to cure. Once identified, you inquire further. Do they give to other causes? If so, how much? Does someone from your nonprofit know them? If you think they may be interested, you *cultivate* them by inviting them to a party, behind-the-scenes tour, or to meet your executive director.

If all goes well, they are then *asked* for a gift, in person, or via email, letter, or phone call. If they give, they are *thanked,* and you attempt to *engage* them more deeply in your cause by asking them to volunteer in some way, perhaps by serving on a committee. You tell them the difference their gift made; that they helped send a child to summer camp or saved a half acre of rain forest.

What Actually Happens

Too often, nonprofits are woefully understaffed. Staff fundraisers may struggle just to keep up with a host of grant proposal deadlines, reports, events, annual and membership appeals, acknowledgments, budgeting, meetings, database management, and their own efforts to research, cultivate, and ask donors.

In the initial step, research, your nonprofit may ask for a list of contacts they can solicit. You may hesitate. You don't want them bothered by your cause, but neither do you want to ask them yourself. You are torn because you know your nonprofit needs money. Let's suppose you overcome your

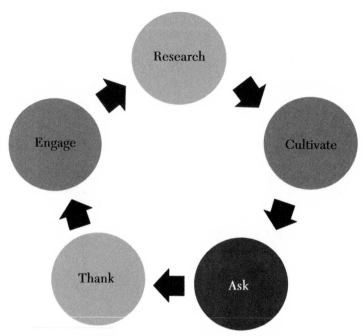

Fig. 1.3. How fundraising should work
©VMJA 2018

reluctance and provide your nonprofit with the names and addresses of some of your friends and colleagues. Your nonprofit adds your folks to their database, flagging you as their solicitor. Later, you may be asked to add handwritten notes to the appeal letters addressed to those you know.

If staff is overwhelmed or there's a turnover in the development office, you may not be told which, if any, of your friends gave in response to your appeal. This can be awkward. When you see them socially, you won't know how to act. If they contributed and you don't mention it, they may assume their gift didn't matter. If they did not give, and you fail to bring it up, they may conclude that you don't care, so they're off the hook. In this no-man's land of ignorance, you may play it safe by avoiding the subject and even the friends you solicited.

Your friends will, of course, continue to get emails, invitations, and appeals from your cause, but if they never hear from you personally, they're unlikely to give again.

Turn the Fundraising Cycle Upside Down

As a nonprofit hero, you'll turn the standard approach to fundraising upside down as illustrated in figure 1.4. You will begin by *thanking*, creatively, personally, and repeatedly, those who already support you, Next, you'll *engage* your donors in ways that enrich their lives. You'll let them know the difference their gift has made and invite them to get more involved.

Do you remember the song from your childhood? *Make new friends but keep the old: one is silver and the other's gold.*

That's why nonprofit heroes spend so much time on current donors.

Any good salesperson will tell you that your best prospects are your current customers. In fundraising, you're selling an opportunity to change the world, rather than computers or a cup of coffee. Developing a base of donors is like building friendships. Most people have lots of acquaintances and a few close friends. No matter how many acquaintances you have, your true friends are the ones who stand by you in good times and bad. Current donors are like those good friends. As a nonprofit hero, you'll concentrate on donors because they know you best, care most, and will be there when you need them.

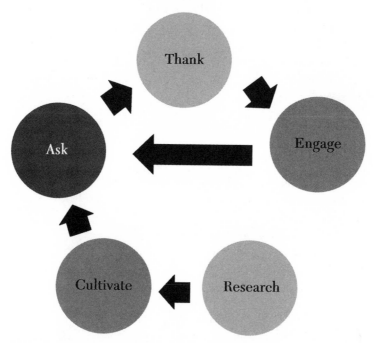

Fig. 1.4. Turn the fundraising cycle upside down
©VMJA 2018

We also begin with current donors because thanking is the easiest part of the ask.

Most of us are far more willing to thank someone than to solicit those who've never given and who (we fear) may slam the door in our face. Thanking is the gentlest part of the fundraising process, gratitude the soil from which much giving springs.

Current donors are worth attending to because they can do much more than write a check. Studies show donors will also volunteer (36 percent), participate in special events (32 percent), help raise funds (29 percent), sign petitions (27 percent), contact legislators on your behalf (20 percent), and tell your story, testifying to your nonprofit's good work (18 percent).

Never a Cold Call

Only when nonprofit heroes have thanked and engaged their current donors well do they turn to *researching, cultivating,* and *asking* prospective donors. Nonprofit heroes take a different approach to contacting prospective donors, for we *never make a cold call.* Why?

The number one reason people give is because someone they know asks them, and they want to help that person. We ask those we know first. Often, this list is so long, we never get around to asking strangers! As we share our enthusiasm for our cause, we'll sense whether our friends and acquaintances wish to learn more. If they do, we can cultivate them, finally asking in a way that fulfills them. Or we may learn this simply isn't one of their interests and move on.

Here's why people give, with the reasons ranked from most compelling to least.[1]

1. Someone I know asked me to give, and I wanted to help them.
2. I felt emotionally moved by someone's story.
3. I want to feel I can help, not feel powerless in the face of need (especially in disasters).
4. I want to feel I'm changing someone's life.
5. I feel a sense of closeness to a community or group.
6. I need a tax deduction.
7. I want to memorialize someone (e.g., who died of a disease or a beloved parent).
8. I was raised to give to charity—it's a tradition in my family.
9. I want to be "hip." Supporting this charity is in style (e.g., colored wrist bands).

10. It makes me feel connected to other people and builds my social network.
11. I want to have a good image for myself/my company.
12. I want to leave a legacy that perpetuates me, my ideals or my cause.
13. I feel fortunate (or guilty) and want to give something back to others.
14. I give for religious reasons: God wants me to share my affluence.
15. I want to be seen as a leader/role model.

We ask for gifts that satisfy donors' desires. Some folks are motivated by just one or two reasons, others by many. Notice that a tax deduction is only the sixth reason on the list. Most people give from the goodness of their hearts. You can help bring this goodness into the world.

Parables

How much do you remember from a self-help book you read five years ago? For most people, the answer is "not much." But you may remember stories, the case studies authors use to illustrate their points. This book uses real-life stories to show you how to fundraise. Each case study (story) is accompanied by a noble attribute, an easy action step, and a quote that illustrates my point more eloquently than I can.

In chapter 2, I'll describe each of the five steps: Thanking, Engaging, Researching, Cultivating, and Asking using the following format:

Case study: I'll relate a story about a step.
Attribute: I'll list a trait/feeling that each step evokes, such as gratitude or creativity.
Saying: I'll share a proverb or maxim; some original, some well known.
Action step: I'll describe one thing you can do, right now, for free, to help raise money.
Quote: I'll close with a quote that reinforces the spirit of each step.

A WORD ABOUT THE STORIES

These stories are all essentially true. I've changed all the names to protect the people and nonprofits I represent. Some are told very nearly as they happened. In other cases, I have combined two or three episodes to make one story. Sometimes, I've put a story that occurred in one kind of setting in a different locale.

Like Aesop, I hope each of my fables conveys a nugget of truth you'll remember.

Fig. 1.5. Aesop's Fables
©iStock.com/duncan1890

❷

THE FIVE STEPS

THANK

We start by thanking (figure 2.1) for several reasons. Most people find it easier to thank donors than to ask them to give. Saying thank you is polite. And thanking is one of the easiest ways to hold on to your current donors.

Donor retention is a crucial issue for nonprofits. Charities *lose more than half their donors (55.5 percent) every year,* according to the 2016 Fundraising Effectiveness Survey Report conducted by the Association of Fundraising Professionals and the Urban Institute.[1] The study found retention among first-time donors was even worse, with only about a quarter (26.6 percent) returning to contribute again. It's expensive to acquire new donors, yet nonprofits must constantly attract new supporters or risk falling behind.

As the Queen of Hearts tells Alice in *Through the Looking-Glass,* "It takes all the running you can do to keep in the same place. If you want to get somewhere else, you must run at least twice as fast as that!"

According to a recent study of donors who'd stopped giving after having made gifts of $250–$2,500 to cultural organizations,[2] not being thanked or acknowledged is the top reason why they stop giving. The second reason they stopped contributing was that no one asked them, and the third that they weren't told how their funds were used.

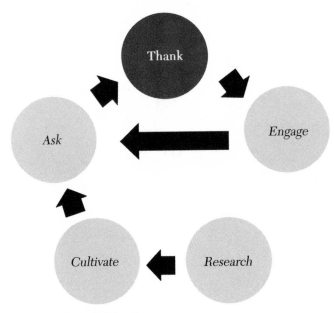

Fig. 2.1. Step 1: Thank
©VMJA 2018

Top Reasons Donors Stopped Giving

1. Not acknowledged or thanked for last gift (19 percent)
2. Not asked to donate again (16 percent)
3. Not told how funds were used (14 percent)
4. Unactualized intent (I forgot) (11 percent)
5. Gave to another charity instead (10 percent)
6. Changing interests/priorities (8 percent)
7. Dissatisfaction with nonprofit (7 percent)
8. Change in finances (couldn't afford) (6 percent)
9. Dissatisfied with use of last gift (5 percent)
10. Asked for too much/too soon after last gift (5 percent)

2016 National Attitudes, Awareness, and Usage Study

Is your nonprofit hemorrhaging donors?

If it is, you may be able to staunch that loss by as much as 33 percent just by thanking donors, personally and well, and telling them what you did with their money. If your charity raises $1 million a year from individuals, that's $330,000 worth of new gifts you *don't* have to find.

Be creative. Thank in whatever way makes you comfortable. If you're social, try thank-a-thons, calls, and visits. If you're more reserved, write heartfelt, handwritten notes. Saying thank you is easy, it's important, and, as your mother taught you, it's the right thing to do.

The Lady Who Talked to Plants

Attribute: *Grateful*
Saying: *Everyone can thank.*
Action Step: *Assign thankers to create and deepen relationships with donors*

The executive director of the Keeley Arboretum of Greenland College was dismayed. She'd had to cancel their seventy-fifth anniversary gala because her council (their equivalent of a board of directors) wasn't buying tickets, priced at seventy-five dollars. This was worrying since the gala was to kick off the arboretum's $3 million campaign for a new education center and greenhouse.

There was no question that the center was desperately needed. Most arboretum volunteers were over sixty years old, many in their eighties. They worked in a leaky, old, badly constructed Quonset hut without heat or air-conditioning. Volunteers froze in the winter and wilted in Philadelphia's humid, 100+ degree summers. The old building could not overwinter plants nor start young ones. Volunteers had no place to store their tools, which were often lost. There was nowhere for the arboretum's hands-on classes, which were, of necessity, wet and dirty.

People who like to garden have many fine qualities. They are often aesthetically sensitive, patient, polite, gracious, far thinking, and gentle. Many are introverted. One told me she'd rather talk to plants than people. The arboretum's council consisted mostly of retired master gardeners, not corporate movers and shakers.

They began by thanking and ended up raising more than 3 million dollars for their gorgeous, new, fully endowed education center and greenhouse.

Here's how it worked. A list of recent donors was distributed at the council's monthly meeting. They reviewed the list, selected names of those they knew, and wrote thank-you notes to those donors. I asked council members to think of something personally meaningful they'd experienced at the arboretum, then to mention that (briefly) in their thank-you notes. There were some donors who no one knew. These names were distributed to those with fewer thanking assignments. Council member Zofia was assigned a $150-donor named Dave, and she wrote a lovely thank-you note, evoking the color and scent of a walk through the arboretum's lilac collection when it was in full bloom.

Fast-forward five months to the arboretum's plant sale.

Now, this is a *serious* plant sale, frequently raising $100,000 or more for the arboretum. Donors are invited to a preview on Friday night, giving them first dibs on plants before the sale opens to the public on Saturday morning.

Dave had RSVP'd to the preview. When he arrived, Zofia was standing next to the check-in table. She introduced herself, thanked him again for his gift, and asked if he was looking for anything special. Dave said yes. He'd just bought a historic farmhouse on three acres. After a forty-five-minute tour and much serious consultation, Dave purchased thousands of dollars' worth of plants and went home happy. Zofia was truly helpful, Dave truly grateful, and each felt they'd made a new friend.

Two months later, Zofia added her personal note to Dave's appeal letter. She asked how his new plants were faring and sent her heartfelt good wishes along with the appeal. Zofia popped the letter in his envelope, sealed it, and wrote her name over the return address, increasing the chances Dave would open it. Dave increased his gift to $1,500, partly because Zofia asked and partly because he'd come to understand and value the arboretum's mission through her.

Zofia became a more willing member of the Capital Campaign Committee once she realized how gentle and congenial fundraising could be. She knew $1,500 gifts from people like Dave wouldn't be enough to raise the millions they needed for the new facility. But the thanking campaign allowed Zofia and other council members to engage in the fundraising process. It lessened their fear and made them realize they could help in small ways. When one volunteer's connections led to a challenge grant, people started believing that the long-planned education center and greenhouse would really be built. Their growing confidence inspired a longtime volunteer to make the $500,000 lead gift that ensured the campaign's success.

"Gratitude is the memory of the heart." French proverb

The Thanking Angel

Attribute:	*Sincere*
Saying:	*Ask once, thank seven times.*
Action step:	*Use thank-a-thons and thank-you note writing parties to spark contagious gratitude.*

Sufism, the mystical branch of Islam, attracts gentle souls. It has few adherents in the United States, but many of those few study or teach at the Spiritual Healing Center (SHC). Most of the SHC board shied away from fundraising and few had any interest in serving on the development committee. The burden fell primarily on one board member, who exhausted himself securing the gifts that made up 75 percent of the center's operating budget. Clearly, this was not sustainable.

I trained their board to ask and helped hire and train development staff to support them. As part of their fundraising makeover, I suggested they appoint a thanking chair to their development committee.

Being spiritually inclined, they assigned a "thanking angel" instead.

Their warmhearted thanking angel, Dana, was also logical, a clear thinker and a sound planner. She was financially sophisticated enough to suggest the center start a planned giving program. She led by example, making a gift of stock that December. She researched the process, understood it, and recommended specific steps for implementation. She wanted to ensure the center's security beyond her term.

But back to thanking.

"Ask once, thank seven times" is a fundraising truism. The thanking angel's job includes ensuring the center's donors are thanked at least seven times for each gift they make. Dana didn't intend to write thousands of thank-you notes herself. Rather, she worked with the development director to harness the immediate and profound gratitude of current students, almost all of whom receive some scholarship. The development director approached a class, asking each student to write a personal thank-you note to a donor. She provided lovely note cards for the purpose and stood back. They wrote with enthusiasm, sharing the many ways the center had changed their lives for the better.

While they were at it, one student asked if he could read his note aloud. Everyone agreed. Then another stood up, and another. As they read their notes, they encouraged and inspired each other. It was contagious. The more they heard, the more grateful they felt. Some students volunteered to write several notes so that they could thank more donors. The recipient donors, all of whom had supported the scholarship fund, were moved to receive such heartfelt thanks, and were inspired by the life-changing impact of their gifts.

"Two logs, when placed together, burn more brightly." Eckhart Tolle

Lucy and the Fair-Trade Network

Attribute:	*Empowering*
Saying:	*Loaves and fishes.*
Action step:	*Recognize and encourage monthly and cumulative giving.*

My daughter Lucy decided she was going to give ten dollars a month to the Fair-Trade Network, since she was committed to healthy food and fair trade. We arranged for ten dollars a month to be deducted from her bank account. She often asked, "Mom, do I have to do more chores? What do I have to do to make sure that money is there for Fair Trade?" Lucy was a twelve-year-old girl with Asperger's syndrome, no one's idea of a major donor, but she gave $360 in three years. Not bad.

You may underestimate some of your smaller donors, thinking, "There's no way they can make a big gift," but if you ask them to give in monthly installments, you may magically convert $20 donors to $200 patrons, $50 givers to $500 contributors. Monthly giving enables people to be more generous. One of your supporters may not be able to write a $1,000 year-end check, but by auto-deducting $100 a month, they can give an even more generous $1,200.

One way of thanking monthly donors is by recognizing cumulative giving. Give your monthly donors a special thank-you and tell them how important it is to you that they are so faithful. In your newsletters, on your website, and in thank-you phone calls, credit donors who achieve a level of giving through monthly deductions.

You should also thank your monthly donors for the steady, predictable, year-round income they provide. Many nonprofits push hard for year-end giving, not knowing until the last moment whether the result will be a balanced budget or a crippling deficit. Monthly giving reduces risk and evens out the usual "feast or famine" cycle of annual giving.

Automated giving plays to a common American weakness: procrastination. Once a donor establishes regular bank deductions, they must actively do something to stop it. Monthly donors are the philanthropic equivalent of frequent flyers. Treat them well and you'll have them forever. Spurn them, and you may lose some of the best friends you've ever had.

How many Lucys are you missing by neglecting to say "Thank you"?

"All difficult things have their origin in that which is easy, and great things in that which is small." Lao Tzu

ACTIVITY: Write One Evocative Thank-You Note

1. Settle in a quiet place and think of one life changed by the gift you're acknowledging.
2. The salutation and postscript (P.S.) are the most read part of a solicitation letter. Get their name right and have a tidbit of time-sensitive info for your P.S.
3. If you know the donor you're thanking, call their image to mind. If not, think of someone you love and write as if to them. It will give your language extra warmth.

Dear [Donor Name]:

Thank you so much for your gift of $X to XYZ Nonprofit. As I write, I can recall [the beneficiary of this gift] vividly, because I visited XYZ Nonprofit just [this morning, last week]. As I approached the [X Facility], I experienced [describe the setting, paint a picture, colors, smells, temperature, sounds, textures, etc.].

I wish you could have seen [describe your personal experience of their gift's impact]. I would be happy to [offer an engaging activity, such as a behind-the-scenes tour] when next you [are in town, visit XYZ Nonprofit.]

Once again, thanks so much for your generosity, and for making [reiterate specific impact] possible.

Sincerely yours,

[Name, Position], XYZ Nonprofit

P.S.: [Add something specific of interest with a date/time and way to RSVP]

[If you need inspiration, turn to the Toolkit section of this book for a sample thank-you note.]

ENGAGE

After you thank donors, you must engage them (figure 2.2). Engagement, also called stewardship, means telling your donors what you did with their money and involving them further. Without engagement, your donor interactions will bounce back and forth between asking and thanking, then asking and thanking again. You may come to remind them of the friend who calls when they want money, gets it, thanks you, then disappears until they need more.

After a while, it wears thin.

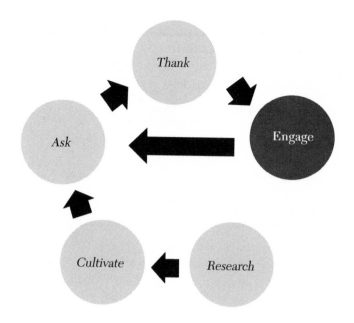

Fig. 2.2. Step 2: Engage
©VMJA 2018

Earlier in this chapter, I shared a study of cultural donors and the reasons why they stopped giving; 14 percent left because they weren't told how their gifts were used. Most charities do a competent job with automated donor communication, sending them newsletters, notices, and invitations to fundraising events. To retain donors, you must both thank them for their last gift and engage them more deeply. Most donors are flattered when board members reach out. For example, if you're attending an event, ask if you'll see the donor there. You may invite them to join you for free events or to volunteer, clearly signaling you want more than just their money. Even if they decline, they may appreciate being asked. These touchpoints give you a chance to discuss the cause you both care about.

Engage your donors consistently, personally, and thoughtfully. You'll distinguish yourself from charities that take them for granted, and you will build longer, deeper, and more satisfying relationships.

The Woman Who Loved Baby Birds

Attribute: *Empathetic*
Saying: *I see you.*
Action step: *Survey donors to find what volunteer activities they'd find most fulfilling, matching person to task if/as possible*

In the science fiction movie *Avatar*, giant blue tribesmen greet each other by saying, "I see you," meaning I see *all* of you, your hopes and fears, who you pretend to be, and who you are, your heart and soul, the true you. It is one person's deeply respectful acknowledgment of another.

After we've thanked a donor, the next step is to engage them more deeply in our mission. You may ask them to serve on a committee, become a docent, host a party, or sign a petition. There are lots of ways to involve donors, but it is important to *see them*. I learned this lesson at the Avian Rescue Center (AVC).

Shanti, a self-effacing, middle-aged woman, came to the AVC asking what she could do to help. She volunteered to care for injured and abandoned birds. A year later, we were delighted when she contributed $5,000. We learned she was wealthy and had connections that could help us tremendously. I suggested we ask her to serve on the development committee with an eye to adding her to the board.

But the board chair, a kind and astute man, was wiser than I. He observed that Shanti was shy, uncomfortable with finances, and none too keen on meetings. He saw how she *loved* baby birds. He understood that tending to them fulfilled her in ways that board service never would. He told me putting Shanti on the board would separate her from the experience that drew her to the center, not bring her closer.

Some baby birds eat every fifteen minutes and must be kept warm round the clock. Shanti volunteered for night shifts, sometimes caring for her demanding avian patients thirty to forty hours a week. She became one of our most knowledgeable volunteers, talking about the birds to anyone who'd listen, including her wealthy friends. She continued to contribute and made a significant planned gift to AVC. Though she never asked for donations, her commitment and passion inspired others to support us.

Our donors are more than checkbooks. If you want them to volunteer, try to engage them in ways that enrich and satisfy them. Avoid creating make-work for wealthy donors. It's a waste of everyone's time. Try to discover what they'll find satisfying and match them to it, at least some of the time.

This is a delicate balance. Volunteers must be trained and supported by staff who are often stretched to the limit. Tasks that one volunteer abhors may satisfy another. Shanti was fine with cleaning baby bird crap. I like structuring databases. Volunteer assignments can build skills, resumes, and friendships. Using your ingenuity and organizational skills to match willing donors to opportunities that will deepen their engagement with your cause.

If you can't afford a volunteer coordinator to do this, consider channeling the skills of that retired executive or hyperorganized volunteer.

"There is no fulfillment in things whatsoever. . . . Having a cause, having a passion . . . that's what gives life's true meaning." Benjamin Carson

The Talking Museum

Attribute:	*Creative*
Saying:	*Find your voice.*
Action step:	*List your engagement activities. Brainstorm more creative approaches if/as needed.*

Half the entries in the museum's sign-in book were illegible. Many visitors wouldn't bother to give their name, and fewer still their email addresses. This was a problem for the Morse Museum, a nonprofit celebrating the life of the painter and inventor Samuel Morse. The sign-in book was the museum's largest source of memberships, and members their largest source of donors.

A friend of the museum is a computer programmer. He looked at the routine task of gathering contact info and came up with an ingenious solution. He envisioned a computer kiosk where visitors could type in their contact info; this alone would improve legibility. His brilliance was that he designed software that made words appear in Morse code as they were typed. Images of dots and dashes would run across the screen. Bursts of short and long clicks would sound with each keystroke.

I have no doubt this will quickly become one of the most engaging exhibits in the museum. School kids will queue up to see their name in Morse code. Adults will be tickled to open Morse email from the museum. The museum will be able to grow its membership, and museum communications will become immediately and intriguingly recognizable. In addition to being distinctive and fun, it's elegantly relevant to the mission.

Once you decide to apply creativity to donor engagement, to speak in your signature voice, a voice no other nonprofit shares, the sky's the limit, literally.

Katie Pastuzek, executive director of Philadelphia's Outward Bound, got our mayor and major donors to rappel down a center city skyscraper. They dramatized the confidence and self-reliance urban kids develop through Outward Bound. The idea was so innovative, she copyrighted it.

Eastern State Penitentiary Historic Site (ESPHS), built in 1829, was once the most famous and expensive prison on earth. Today it's a ruin, a haunting world of crumbling cell blocks and empty guard towers. The penitentiary's *Terror Behind the Walls* is a Halloween haunted "house" that draws more than 100,000 visitors each fall and generates half of ESPHS's annual income. They once allowed supporters who donated $1,000 to portray one of *Terror*'s ghouls, with a specific character's backstory, makeup, costume, and haunting territory. I suspect donors learned more prison history by playing these characters than they ever would by attending lectures or reading brochures.

Ask yourself, "What can we do that no one else can do? What unforgettable experience can we give our donors? How can we engage them with a voice that's uniquely our own?"

"Creativity is putting your imagination to work." Sir Ken Robinson

My Favorite Accountant

Attribute: *Impactful*

Saying: *How did I change the world?*

Action step: *Start meeings with one vivid experience or memorable impact step.*

Jim, a senior executive at his accounting firm, chaired the development committee of Board Benefit (BB). He was utterly convinced of its value to the entire region. As an alumnus, he had seen the profound impact it had on his life, and that of his classmates. He was a fearless, cheerful, enthusiastic, engaging, and deeply authentic asker.

He was such a star that I made him my guinea pig for a board training on donor engagement. I knew he'd rise to the occasion (and probably forgive me afterward). I asked Jim to imagine that I was Josie W., who'd contributed $2,500 last year. Here's how it went.

Val: What did Board Benefit do with my money? What difference did I make?

Jim: You helped us balance the budget.

Val: What difference did I make?

Jim: Um, well, you helped us pay Cynthia's salary. Cynthia is our alumni relations officer. She helps match trained alumni to nonprofits looking for board members.

Val: What difference did I make?

Jim thought harder.

Jim: The zoo's outreach grew, because one of our alumni, Susie V., joined its board.

Val: What difference did I make?

Pause.

Jim's a smart man and extremely good with figures. He cast his mind back over the last year, made a quick calculation, smiled, and addressed me as if I were the donor.

Jim: A twelve-year-old girl from one of Philly's worst schools went from failing science to acing it. She wants to become a biologist because of you. She got to attend the zoo's summer camp, a program BB alum Susie V. has championed. If you'd contributed $2,500 to the zoo scholarship fund, this girl would've gone to camp, but it would have ended there. Our alumnus is using her BB skills to connect people to resources in ways that will ignite this girl's interest in science this year, and that of hundreds of other girls and boys in the years ahead.

Val: Wow! My $2,500 made a big difference!

It wasn't fair to ask Jim such a question. In real life, Board Benefit's staff would have prepped him. But I'm sure you get the point, as Jim did. If you know the impact someone's $25, $100, or $10,000 contribution made, tell them. If you don't know, ask.

After all, why should they give a dollar if nothing changes?

"Man is the only animal that laughs and weeps, for only he . . . is struck by the difference between what things are and what they ought to be."
William Hazlitt (1778–1830)

My Anasazi Summer

Attribute:	*Honorable*
Saying:	*I am not an ATM.*
Action Step:	*Create your own impact story journal and add to it regularly.*

I had to drop out of Hamilton College, and I just couldn't bear it. I was a junior and had to fulfill my archaeology summer field work requirement to get my B.A. I ached to go on a dig, but it was unpaid. I worked a part-time job during the school year and a full-time one each summer. Without my summer earnings, I couldn't afford to pay my senior year tuition.

The summer before I'd worked two full-time jobs, teaching theater to thirty excited kids by day and toiling at a textile factory's clattering looms by night. I'd bike to the theater in the morning, teach children all day, bike home, eat, sleep, bike to the factory for my 11 p.m. shift, work, bike home in the morning, shower, eat, and bike to the theater to start all over again. I was exhausted, knew I couldn't work any harder, and didn't know what to do.

I wasn't really paying attention as I sat, glumly, at Hamilton's Class and Charter Day that spring. My dejected musings were interrupted by the announcement of my name.

Stunned, I walked up to the podium to accept a scholarship I didn't know existed and hadn't applied for. It was designed to "expand the scope of a scholar's education beyond Hamilton's curriculum." It covered the whole summer's costs *and* fall tuition. Walking back to my seat, I wondered how this could have happened, until I spied my anthropology professors peering at me from the faculty section.

They looked very smug.

Aha!

That summer, I rose at dawn, bathed in near-frigid water, and used a latrine. I worked atop a 1,000-foot-high mesa, scraping at barely differentiated layers of rock-hard dirt. The view from my perch was vast, but sometimes, my world shrank to a few square feet encompassed by string. I once spent days working a patch, only to get a laconic "nope" from the dig boss, who told me to cover it up again.

I wasn't discouraged. I loved it. Because I was finally on an adventure.

One day, I was excavating a fire pit. I'd stick my blade in, pry, pop out a chunk of charcoal. Stick my blade in, pry, pop out another bit. Stick my blade in, pry and . . . a cylinder of turquoise flew up toward the sun, and I had a sudden vision.

Nighttime, silhouetted shapes sitting around the fire. A young girl prancing. She's dusky, laughing, chest bare but for a rough necklace. Suddenly, the cord breaks and beads fly. A single turquoise tube tumbles into the flames. Her mouth forms a startled "O" of loss.

Then I was back, surrounded by dirt, trowels, and string. The bead was in my hand, and I clung to it. Closing my eyes, I saw her again, *so* vividly. I reported my find, duly marking the bead's position on the graphed site map, sealing it in a tiny plastic bag, labeling it, and putting it with the other artifacts. I found no more beads that day or later. But I wondered: Who sent me here? What unknown donor positioned me to catch a gem that pierced time?

I wrote Hamilton and learned that a college trustee had once asked two sisters to make a gift. They said yes, establishing "my" scholarship in honor of their father, an alumnus. I wrote the two now-elderly ladies, care of Hamilton College Development Office. Just a postcard introducing myself and thanking them for funding my fieldwork. They wrote back, telling me no recipient had ever thanked them. Not once in forty years. Thrilled to be included in my grand undertaking, they thanked *me* profusely. We began an illicit correspondence, outside official college channels.

I described impossible sunsets and snow in July, kivas, cliff-dwellings, and a hawk shrieking her mastery of an infinite blue sky. I told them of the girl-child's bead, lost until it forged a brief, electric bridge through time. They told me about their dad, their lives, and their accomplishments. I told them my hopes and fears. They gave me advice so wise I didn't understand it for decades.

How is it possible that turquoise can time travel, but I was the first recipient to tell these donors what I did with their money?

Some nonprofits treat donors like ATMs, going to them for money again and again, but not engaging them between withdrawals. Your donors give because they want to make a difference, so *tell them* the difference that they made! They'll give more generously, more often, and, most important, with joy. They deserve the satisfaction of knowing the good work they've funded. Repay their generosity in the coin of impact stories.

As a board member, you can tell your donors about the difference their gift makes. Focus on the impact on *one* person's (or one animal's) life. Save the statistics for later. You can ask staff for stories, but you'll tell a more powerful story if you experience it yourself.

Sit in on a program the donor funded. If it's a healthy cooking class for urban children, try it yourself! Go to the elder-center when a computer class is in session or music lessons for disadvantaged youth. I like to start each board meeting with an experience or an impact story, told, if possible, by the person who benefitted. Try journaling these stories so that you can capture, remember, and convey in your own words the impact each gift makes.

"My hope is to leave the world a little better for my having been here." Jim Henson

ACTIVITY: Impact Story Journaling

1. List one of your nonprofit's programs you find most important (e.g., its summer camp).

———————————————————————————————

2. Describe one person (or animal) whose life was changed for the better. Age? Hair color? Eyes? Build? Situation that brought them to your nonprofit? If you don't know, ask. If staff can't tell you, sit in on a program and learn for yourself. Imagine you're a reporter.

———————————————————————————————

———————————————————————————————

———————————————————————————————

3. Now describe the setting. What time was it? Light or dark? Moist or dry? Indoor or out? Textures, colors, sounds, smells?

———————————————————————————————

———————————————————————————————

———————————————————————————————

4. What changed? "An elderly woman got three computer literacy lessons" is good. That's called an output. Try describing *impact*: "She'd never even gotten a card from her grandson. She sent her first email, and he replied in minutes. She was so thrilled she almost cried. She's

less isolated, less lonely, and more connected to her friends and family."

_____

_____

_____

_____

Once you've captured the experience, you can work backward to figure out the cost, and thus the gift level that made that impact.

RESEARCH

The purpose of research (figure 2.3) is to get to know current donors better, to discover likely donors, and to rule out those unlikely to support your cause.

Your nonprofit database is your repository of internal donor information. It should tell you how much they've contributed, for how long, and whether they support any special initiatives. It should note who knows them and the donor's involvement with your organization, whether they've volunteered or attended events. It should provide you with notes from anyone who has solicited them in the past. Shockingly, *one in five nonprofits has no fundraising database at all.*[3] Before collecting new information, make sure you have captured and can manage what you already know.

For both current and prospective donors, you'll also want relevant external data, such as how much they give to other organizations, their jobs, assets, and possible interest in your cause. For example, if you're a theater, you might want to know if a prospect acted in college. If your nonprofit's mission is to cure a dreaded disease, you might wish to know if someone in

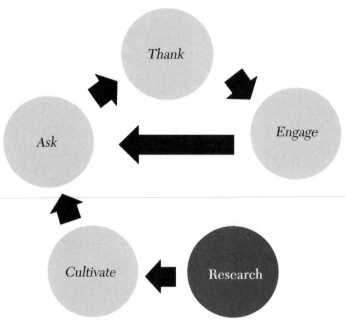

Fig. 2.3. Step 3: Research
©VMJA 2018

their family suffers from that condition. If you, as a board member, know the person in question, you can provide guidance that's not found online. For example, you might know that it's a bad time to ask because they're going through a divorce, or a good one because they're about to take the family business public.

Staff can help you organize prospect rating sessions. In these, you'll develop the best approach for current donors, review lists of members and contributors to peer nonprofits, and try to find contacts with corporate executives and/or foundation trustees. Speak of others as you'd like to be spoken of. The goal is to find those who will want to give, not to gossip. If you're unsure, check www.afpnet.org/files/ContentDocuments/Donor_Bill_of_Rights.pdf, the Donor Bill of Rights.

Make research an ongoing activity, not an occasional event, and involve everyone—staff, board, and volunteers—in generating a year-round stream of new funding sources.

Stars over the Caribbean

Attribute:	*Optimistic*
Saying:	*Inhabit a friendly universe.*
Action step:	*Assign an optimistic reader to generate a constant flow of new prospects.*

We'd arrived at that perfect mid-vacation moment. Our relaxed, Caribbean selves had left our wintry selves far behind. The seafood shack where we'd dined glowed golden behind us. Ahead, waves slapped and tickled the shore, luring us on. A pier of silky wooden planks held the day's warmth, so we stretched out. At first, we lay in silent harmony, digesting.

Side by side, on our backs, we contemplated the parade of stars. They bore little resemblance to their northern sisters, those dim glimmers that struggled through light pollution to reach us. Here, we watched the pathway of the gods, a glorious carpet of stars stretching from horizon to horizon. Shooting stars flew by so fast that by the time our brains registered their presence, they were gone. We watched a take-no-prisoners, gorgeously brilliant night sky.

"Wow," I said, with remarkable originality. "Don't you want to dive in and go swimming in that sea of stars?"

"No," said my husband. "I'm afraid I'd be sucked into the cold void of outer space and lost forever. I need to hold tight to this pier and not let go."

For some, the universe is a dangerous enemy. For others, it's welcoming, full of friends to meet and as-yet undiscovered wonders.

You can decide that no one cares about your cause. You can assume they will reject it (and you) if asked for support. If you're right, the world of fundraising is fraught with peril. If, on the other hand, you believe your life is ablaze with human stars twinkling brightly, ready to light your way . . . well, then, fundraising's a grand adventure. There are as many generous humans as there are stars in a tropical night sky.

I know, because I've met so many of them.

What do you believe?

If you need to identify new donors, I suggest you assign an optimistic reader, someone who can scan the news for the human stars who might fund your cause.

The reader's job is to identify those who might care about your mission. Someone in the know. Board members in marketing and sales make good readers, as do those whose work requires them to be aware of community leaders. News junkies, those people who devour several papers a day and watch CNN for fun, are often very good at this.

Let's say your nonprofit provides music lessons for children. Your reader may catch an interview with an entrepreneur who wanted to be a concert violinist. The reader doesn't have to know the entrepreneur nor research him or her. Their job is to seek, find, and pass on the names of possible supporters. A staff member or intern can research these prospects further, ranking each, and adding the most promising to your database.

Your mission won't resonate with all those you identify. An important research goal is to winnow out those unlikely to fall in love with your cause, the better to focus on those who will. Some of the prospects you identify will care enough to give, and a handful will become advocates and champions, donating for decades to come.

Keep scanning the heavens, and you'll build your own constellation of star supporters.

"The most important decision we make as human beings is whether we live in a friendly or hostile universe, and whichever way we decide, that becomes true." Albert Einstein

The Fond Grandfather

Attribute:	*Observant*
Saying:	*Hidden in plain sight.*
Action Step:	*As a board, review lists of new members, donors, and visitors . . . often!*

Only the hardiest families visit northern zoos in January, so I figured it wouldn't take long to review that week's list of new members. It didn't, so I did. The Woods Zoo only had one fundraiser, Jane. She'd done the work of two to three people since her boss had left nearly a year earlier. I knew Jane didn't have the time, but what about the board? They were the town's movers and shakers, the zoo's ambassadors who knew everybody. They'd not been asked to review the list of those who joined each month either.

As I looked at the names, twelve memberships one week, nineteen the next, I couldn't help looking them up online. I'm compulsive that way (and curious). I discovered a member mom worked for Comcast. A new member dad did marketing for the electric company. I added their names as possible contacts for each corporation. Week by week, I identified a pool of insiders who were friendly to the zoo, who could provide guidance and support when we applied to their companies for funding.

When Mr. Anthony Carrefour bought a grandparent membership for himself and Tiffany, I knew I'd hit pay dirt. If the board had reviewed membership lists, they might have recognized him as well. He'd just donated $10 million to a science museum. He could afford to buy tickets for the day. That he purchased a membership suggested he wanted to come often, that the time he spent at the zoo with his granddaughter was important to him.

The zoo is cultivating Mr. Carrefour to see if he wants to get more involved. They are getting to know him (and vice versa) and haven't yet asked for a gift. But he's certainly a prospect who likes the zoo, lives nearby, wants children to be science literate, and can help them in a big way.

I've spent a lot of my life looking at donor lists and attending galas. The more you do it, the better you get. But I didn't know the donors in this community, whereas the zoo's board did. They would have recognized the head of the local car dealership, the up-and-coming attorney, the soon-to-retire CEO, and the wealthy, philanthropic entrepreneur who was also a grandpa.

The donors you need may be sitting next to you, reading to a child, applauding the show, or rescuing an abandoned pup.

Make sure you don't miss the prospects hidden in plain sight.

"Go within or go without." Buddhist saying

My Mechanic's Buddy

Attribute:	*Connected*
Saying:	*Friends before strangers.*
Action step:	*Use LinkedIn to connect with members of your nonprofit's board and staff.*

I knew I'd find someone to introduce me to Chambers Subaru. As I looked through my thousands of contacts I found I had access in practically every industry . . . except cars.

How did *that* happen?

I thought and thought, wanting to help my client while sticking to my "no cold calls" rule. I plugged "Chambers Subaru" into my LinkedIn account and saw Joe was connected. Of course! I'd taken my Subaru to Joe for service for years. I contacted Joe, reminded him of who I was, and explained the situation. He couldn't have been nicer. He told me the executive who handled sponsorship wasn't Mr. Chambers senior, but rather his son.

"Do you know the son?" I asked.

"Yeah," Joe laughed, "I was his buddy in high school."

Joe reviewed the zoo's Subaru sponsorship package and made excellent suggestions. He provided an e-introduction to the younger Mr. Chambers and, after some back and forth, he toured the zoo. He got a quiet stroll during a hectic workweek. He saw schoolchildren in a biology lesson, the size of the parking lot that would fill with cars in the summertime, and learned about the demographics of our members. He shared their marketing strategy with me, so I understood why they declined to sponsor our new exhibit.

I wasn't discouraged.

He'd gotten to know us and made an informed decision. Had I mailed the sponsorship package, he might never have seen the zoo, learned about our programs, or understood how much marketing muscle we brought to the table. But he came. And who knows? We might partner with Chambers Subaru in the future.

It's more efficient to identify a few prospects where you have a connection than to send a thousand letters that end up in the trash, unopened and unread. One of the easiest ways to find an intermediary is through social networks like LinkedIn. Connect with your peers on the board, on staff, and/or with fellow volunteers. Through the magic of multiplication, you'll soon have access to thousands of second- and third-degree connections, ensuring that you, like me, will never have to make a cold call.

"Only connect . . . and both will be exalted." E. M. Forster

A Very Small Town

Attribute: *Curious*

Saying: *Do your homework.*

Action step: *Get and read prospects' bios to identify possible connections.*

Greenland is an idyllic little village, inhabited by commuting professionals, gentle academics, and Greenland College students. Elderly couples still worship in churches they joined as newlyweds. Kids ride decorated fire engines on the Fourth of July. Everyone knows your name, as well as the name of the folks who owned your house before you. It's a small town.

Just on the other side of the highway from Greenland lies Widnertown, where unemployment is high, educational achievement low, and the average male life expectancy a scant fifty-seven years. The Widnertown Children's Chorus (WCC) bridges this gulf with the shared language of music, inspiring and transforming hundreds of children's lives.

Most of the chorus's board of directors live in Greenland. They are smart, active, engaged, and connected. I'd identified several new foundation prospects for the board to review. I was particularly excited about the Martin Foundation. It was located nearby and had made $100,000+ grants to fund music outreach for disadvantaged children. The foundation listed no staff and only three trustees: Mr. and Mrs. Martin and John Griffith. Application to the foundation was by invitation only, but no one on WCC's board knew the foundation trustees. It seemed like a nonstarter.

But it was *such* a good prospect, I couldn't give up. I read the bios of the Martins, the husband and wife who endowed the foundation. I also reread the bios of all the Widnertown Children's Chorus's board members. No obvious connection.

But what about Mr. Griffith? I found he was an attorney. Further investigation revealed that he served on the board of a community theater. The theater? The Players Club of *Greenland.*

As I said, it's a very small town.

I went back to the chorus's board.

"Do you know anyone involved with the Players Club?" I inquired.

"I know three people on that board."

"My husband ran lights for their last show."

"My daughter's been going to their summer camp for years."

Once the WCC board realized they had connections in common with a foundation trustee, they sprang into action. An introduction was quickly arranged. Mr. Griffith agreed to attend the chorus's next concert. Their rendering of Mozart's Requiem impressed him greatly, and the foundation invited the chorus to submit a proposal. I do not know if the chorus will be funded. I know my curiosity combined with the chorus board's connections, opened a $100,000 door that would otherwise have been closed to us.

"The cure for boredom is curiosity.
There is no cure for curiosity." Dorothy Parker

ACTIVITY: Identify Board Connections to New Corporate Funders through LinkedIn

Part 1. The more active your board and staff are on LinkedIn, the more useful this will be.

A. Get the list of your fellow board members.
B. Invite them to LinkedIn, explaining that this will help your nonprofit identify connections to current and prospective donors.
C. Get the list of your nonprofit's senior staff and invite them as well.

Part 2. Wait a few weeks to allow folks to accept your invitations.

A. Select two to three companies you'd like to approach for your non-profit.
B. Go to each company's LinkedIn profile. It should tell you "## of this company's employees are on LinkedIn; you are connected to ## employees."
C. Those you're connected to: You might know the friends/colleagues who work for these companies, but you may be surprised to learn you have connections you hadn't thought of, such as a fellow Little League parent.
D. Let's say you don't have any first-degree connections. Click on the list of all the company's employees and select second-degree con-nections. This means you know someone who knows someone at that company, someone who could introduce you.

Part 3. Bring your list of connections to your next board or development committee meeting and ask your peers to do the same. Chances are good one of you will have a connection to the funder you want to approach.

CULTIVATE

You date before you get married, research a mutual fund before investing, and visit colleges before applying. Like you, donors want to get to know your nonprofit before contributing. The purpose of cultivation is for both parties to discern if it's a match. You want to know who is willing and able to give. Ideally, you want to find those who'll fall in love with your nonprofit and become lifetime donors.

So how do you do that?

It depends on your nonprofit, your prospective donor, and you. A shelter for battered women does not have the same cultivation opportunities a theater can offer. A hands-on donor might need to work in a soup kitchen to fathom the impact of hunger, while an analytical donor might grasp it by reading a report. An extravert may connect with prospects in social situations, while an introvert does better one-on-one or in writing.

The wonderful thing about cultivation is that prospects are self-selecting. If you invite ten friends to a dawn hike in the wetlands, you'll soon discover

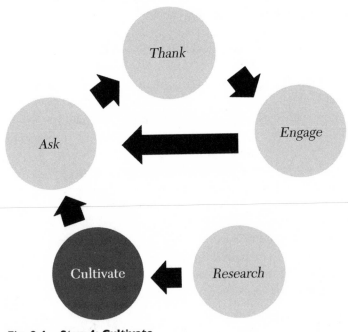

Fig. 2.4. Step 4: Cultivate
©VMJA 2018

which of your buddies is a nature lover, or at least who is (or is not) a morning person. Cultivating others yields advantages to the cultivator. After all, if you invite others to a lecture, you must attend yourself and will learn more about your nonprofit as a result.

Boa in the Boardroom

Attribute:	*Vibrant*
Saying:	*Nothing sells the zoo like the zoo.*
Action Step:	*In addition to dollar goals, set site visit goals that offer memorable experiences.*

I was the only zoo administrator who'd taken the animal handling course, and I decided to use it.

I was charged with securing corporate, foundation, and government funding and with supporting the corporate committee. It was made up of twelve businessmen (they were all men at the time) who'd volunteered to raise funds for the zoo. I structured agendas, drafted their letters and brochures, and developed prospect lists. Earnest and dutiful as they were, their fundraising assignments often slipped to the bottom of their to-do lists.

I set up the boardroom as usual. Agendas and supporting materials lay in folders, neatly labeled with the name of each committee member. I chatted briefly with each arrival as they assembled, before excusing myself.

A few minutes later, I reentered the meeting.

I was well accessorized, with a five-foot-long python named Lulu draped across my shoulders.

I learned one thing fast. Some people don't like snakes.

Chairs toppled as committee members fled to the far wall or under the table. Slowly they emerged. I told one gentleman he had nothing to fear from her fangs, as ball pythons have no venom and rarely bite unless provoked. I explained that, far from being a man-eater, Lulu dined mostly on rats. They seemed to calm when I mentioned that, when threatened, she had an adorable habit of rolling into a ball and tucking her head in the middle! I spent a few minutes correcting other misunderstandings. No, ball pythons didn't inhabit the Amazonian rain forest, but rather the open forests and dry grasslands of Africa.

I taught the braver committee members find to use two fingers to stroke the back of Lulu's head. Some were surprised to her skin was dry, not slimy. They learned that ball pythons have a special sense that allows them to detect infrared temperature change of only 3/1,000 of a degree. This, when combined with their excellent vision, allows them to find their prey in the dark.

Though not endangered, the ball python is threatened. In one year alone, 45,000 ball pythons were exported from Ghana and Togo, bound for U.S. pet stores. Many die before they reach our shores or shortly thereafter, due to negligent or ignorant pet owners. Habitat destruction and tourist demand for python-skin souvenirs further diminish wild python populations. I used Lulu to explain the plight of other endangered snakes and emphasized what the zoo was doing to protect them. I returned Lulu to her cage, and we proceeded with the agenda.

Committee members left with an exciting anecdote to share with their colleagues, friends, relatives, and even acquaintances. These gents could have read everything they learned from me on the zoo website, but their vivid experience that day ensured they understood it more deeply and retained what they'd learned.

Over the next weeks and months, they spread the zoo's conservation message with an infectious enthusiasm that was hard to deny. Some still mentioned it a year later. Five years later, a committee member hailed me across a crowded ballroom, with, "Hey, snake lady!"

Like many nonprofits, the zoo asked each member of the corporate development committee to raise a certain amount of money each year. We kept those "get" goals, adding a *site visits* goal. They each agreed to bring five prospects to behind-the-scenes zoo visits. And they did, frequently asking to visit Lulu so they could tell their guests the story of their first encounter with her.

The site visit prospects screened themselves. If they weren't interested in animals or zoos, they declined. Those who came were genuinely interested. As they toured the zoo, we listened, noting which animals they liked and what programs intrigued them. The more friends our committee members brought, the more comfortable they became. The more comfortable the committee grew, the more frequently they asked their guests to give and the more money they raised.

Your cultivation activities should catch and hold prospects' attention. They provide a platform for highlighting the best of what you do and what, with their help, you hope to achieve. Though engagement and cultivation activities are similar, their purpose is slightly different. We hope to bring *donors* closer to an organization they already support, so that they become involved insiders. The purpose of cultivating *prospects* is to introduce them to your nonprofit, to see if they are interested, and, if so, to better understand how giving to your nonprofit might satisfy them.

Cultivation activities must adhere to rules (e.g., participant safety). Take care to avoid overburdening staff. Given a little lead time, most nonprofit employees are eager to share their work with prospective funders. Focus on site visit goals, and the dollars will follow.

And who knows who (or what) may appear in *your* boardroom!

"May you live all the days of your life." Jonathan Swift

What I Learned Saying Good-Bye

Attribute: *Receptive*
Saying: *Catch them coming and going.*
Action step: *Station "farewellers" to speak to people as they leave your events.*

I learned a lot from Rector Randy when I served on the vestry of our church.

For example, as stewardship chair, I was trying to figure how we might increase contributions. I noticed that we had many "member" families I'd never met and who never gave. "Look at all these prospects!" I said. "We should be soliciting them."

"Val," Randy replied, "If I spent my time on everyone who didn't come to church, I'd have a congregation full of them."

Meaning, of course, that the church would be empty.

Randy also taught me the importance of connecting with people as they *left* the church.

We had greeters and ushers to welcome parishioners. They'd whisper hello as they handed out programs for the service and seated them.

After the last hymn ended, Randy stood by the exit, chatting to everyone who stopped for a word. Those in a hurry left by another door, but most of the congregation queued up. One by one, they shook hands, Randy asked after their families; they shared news, complimented him on his sermon, or asked questions.

The entire congregation. One by one. Week after week. Year after year.

I watched him build relationships with parishioners, one farewell at a time.

People coming into an event are eager to get seated and served. Though some may be in a hurry to leave, many make leisurely exits, reflecting on what they've experienced, willing to share their thoughts about a speaker or program.

Try stationing a board member or volunteer at the exit of each of your events or performances. Have them ask how your visitors enjoyed their experience. Answer the questions you can. If you can't, take their contact info and offer get back to them. It's a wonderful and nonthreatening way to engage constituents and get to know them better.

"Why struggle to open a door
between us when the whole wall is an illusion?" Rumi

ACTIVITY: Match Cultivation Activities to Donors/Friends

- List cultivation activities you're planning to attend, ones you find fun/interesting.
- List three people/funders who might be interested in each activity.
- List dates/cost. If not free, agree in advance who'll pay for your guests.

If you need inspiration, you'll find a completed cultivation chart in the Toolkit section of this book.

Table 2.1. Cultivation Activity Chart (Blank) © VMJA 2018

Cultivation activity	List three people you could invite	Activity date(s)	Is it free or will it cost?	If it costs, who will pay?
A.	1. 2. 3.			
B.	1. 2. 3.			
C.	1. 2. 3.			

ASK

By the time you get to the fifth step, ask (figure 2.5), you should know that the person you're approaching is willing to help. If they're donors, you'll have thanked and engaged them well enough to know they're ready to give. If you're asking prospects, you'll have researched and cultivated them enough to know they have the interest, capacity, and desire to support your cause.

Few people meet with you to say no.

They just decline the visit. If they agree to discuss their support of your cause, they're usually planning to say yes. Remember, the number one reason people give is because someone they know asked them and they wanted to help. And one of the most frequent reasons they stop giving is because no one asked them!

The asking stories below include some inspirational successes as well as a cautionary tale of how not to ask.

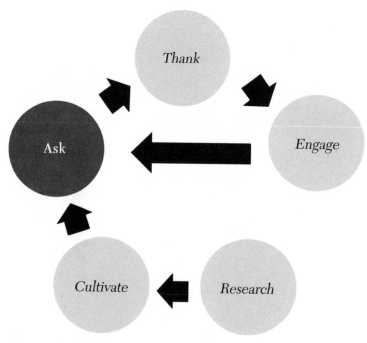

Fig. 2.5. Step 5: Ask
©VMJA 2018

Asking isn't a performance; it's a conversation. You should listen as much, or more, than you talk. Most donors are on your side and are as anxious as you are to have your visit go well. You're there to enable your donor to make a difference, to change the world for the better, to leave their mark.

A good day's work, by any measure.

Zoo vs. Dallas Theater

Attribute:	*Generous*
Saying:	*Lead by example.*
Action step:	*Give first yourself, generously and thoughtfully, before asking others.*

In the early 1990s, I made a modest salary working for a zoo as director of corporate, foundation, and government relations. Before I asked anyone else, I had to give myself, so I dug deep, pledging $300 over three years, a significant gift for me at that time.

A few years later, I started a new position as director of development for the Dallas Theater, an African American theater and performing arts training program. The Dallas had a robust staff giving campaign, and I decided to lead by example. I was proud of myself for pledging $500 in just one year. Proud, that is, until my fellow department heads, many of whom earned less than me, *pledged $1,000 a year to the Dallas.* It taught me how profoundly committed they were to the Dallas and to the work they were doing.

I had given generously, and I am not suggesting that you, as a board member, should give sacrificially or in ways that might harm your families. I am suggesting you should give more than you would if you were not a board member. You are responsible for the health and well-being of your nonprofit and must set an example. After all, you wouldn't ask someone else to feed your children, would you?

And here's a tip. The more generously you give, the more confident you will be in asking, and the more willing to ask for larger gifts.

"We get no more than we have been willing to risk giving." Sheldon Kopp

Mrs. Johnson

Attribute: *Confident*

Saying: *Don't put your toddler on a Harley.*

Action step: *Have board members ask three donors before one nondonor.*

I was at the Dallas Theater working with one of the wealthiest African American women in her community. Mrs. Johnson was a private and reserved person. I asked her to help me with a few prospective donors whom only she could ask. She dreaded the very thought of fundraising, but she reluctantly agreed. She came to my office so that I could prepare her to ask Mr. Dwayne Robbins for a gift. Even though we rehearsed the entire visit, she was so nervous she had her brother drive her to see Mr. Robbins.

After she left me, I called Dwayne, who regularly gave $1,500 a year.

I said, "Dwayne, Mrs. Johnson is on her way to ask you for a gift to the Dallas Theater. When she does, I'd like you to contribute $2,000."

He said, "What! I never give more than $1,500."

I said, "I know, but Mrs. Johnson is terrified you'll turn her down. We just spent an hour practicing. Please stretch a bit and give her a nice surprise."

Dwayne said, "I would never say no to Mrs. Johnson. So, what is she going to say?"

I told him. Dwayne asked, "What else is she going to say?"

And I told him. Then he said, "OK, when she says that, I can say this . . .and then do you think it would be good if I told her this?" And I said, "Yeah, that would be great. Good idea. And don't forget to tell her about the time your son was taking acting class and . . ." And so on.

By the end of our call, Dwayne was conspiring to help Mrs. Johnson ask *him* to give.

Later that afternoon, I got a call from Mrs. Johnson. "You won't believe it," she said. "He gave me $2,500! Val, it turns out that I'm a *great* fundraiser!"

And she was right.

I made sure Mrs. Johnson's next visits were to donors who had given before and would give again, at some level. By her fourth success, Mrs. Johnson had the confidence to ask a lapsed donor, then someone who had never given. One of those individuals was a person I'd originally earmarked as someone whom she, and only she, could solicit.

You wouldn't put a toddler on a Harley Davidson . . . you'd start them on a tricycle.

Yet board members are often told, "We don't need you to ask those who already support us. We need you to get your friends who know nothing about us, to give."

As a board member, ask to solicit current donors. Once you've got several gifts and thousands of dollars under your belt, you'll discover, as Mrs. Johnson did, that you're a *great* fundraiser.

"Life shrinks or expands in proportion to one's courage." Anais Nin

Pitching Hollywood

Attribute:	*Inspired*
Saying:	*Always have a backup.*
Action step:	*Develop two to three funding ideas for each major donor you visit*

There's a famous story about two writing partners, screenwriters who'd spent months getting a meeting to pitch their idea for a movie. Finally, the big day came. They'd barely spoken two sentences when the movie mogul interrupted.

"Nah, I don't like it. Got anything else?"

Pause.

"Yes, of course we do," they said, improvising. "It's a story about two guys . . . creative guys, and about their wives and kids." They went on to describe their lives, and those of their friends and family. On the spot, they created an award-winning movie that captured the essence of an era.

But few of us are as good at improvising.

Don't assume that because you've read your donor's bio and giving history, you know all about them. You don't. They may have just read an article about hunger or learned a family member was diagnosed with cancer. They may be studying violin, an instrument they hadn't picked up since childhood. Feeding the hungry, fighting cancer, and teaching music are all causes worth supporting. They just may not be what you'd planned on pitching.

You can't know for sure what will motivate your donor, but you can be prepared. In addition to the initiative that seems right up their alley, try to think of one or two other projects they might like. Doing so will cause you to see your donor more holistically, listen more attentively, and respond more genuinely. Do your homework, but don't get too stuck on preconceived notions of what they'll want. And if they ask, "Have you got anything else?" at least you'll have a backup plan.

> *"It is better to be prepared for an opportunity and not have one,*
> *than to have one and not be prepared."*
> Whitney Young, Jr.

The Crabby Advocate

Attribute:	*Transformative*
Saying:	*Spend words before money.*
Action step:	*Keep your sense of humor and stay open to the possibility of positive outcomes, even from difficult conversations.*

We were reviewing lists of prospective donors to the Keeley Arboretum of Greenland College's capital campaign. "How about this gentleman?" I asked. Our notes indicated he was an alumnus, understood horticulture, and owned cranberry bogs that, when sold for development, would make him a very wealthy man. In terms of assets and understanding, he seemed like an excellent prospect to me.

Unfortunately, Mr. Kravitz was a grumpy old man. He complained about everything and was furious at the college for closing its football program. Though he'd made small gifts to the arboretum, no one wanted to solicit him, including Crystal, the executive director.

One brave board member, Susan, stepped forward, and we decided she and I would visit him. When I called to set the appointment, he said, "You know I'm not going to give you any money." And I said, "What you choose to do is completely up to you. We'd just like an opportunity to speak with you." He agreed, a bit huffily, muttering, "You're not getting a dime," before hanging up.

When Susan and I arrived on the appointed day, she opened the conversation by asking if he had any concerns about Greenland College or the Keeley Arboretum. His eyes lit up and he launched into his tirade: "Let me tell you what's wrong with those idiots at the college. . . ." After a forty-five-minute rant about the college's shortcomings, he wound down.

It was my turn.

I asked if he had any *other* objections, and, once again, he was off. We listened to him vent for another fifteen minutes. Then Susan said, "I think you might be interested in two aspects of the Education Center and Greenhouse project. . . ." She listed advantages for overwintering and back-friendly workstations for elderly volunteers.

"Do you think you could help underwrite one of these?" Susan asked sweetly.

"Nope," he retorted, obviously enjoying himself.

We thanked him for his time and left him a beautiful brochure describing the planned center. "If you change your mind," said Susan earnestly, "let us know."

Three years went by, and the campaign was wrapping up. We still needed several major gifts to make our goal. Looking through the remaining prospects, we saw his name. Crystal, the executive director, looked at us, we looked at her, and she said, "No. Oh, no. There is no way I'm making that call!"

But Susan was game, and so was I. Once again, I called to set the appointment. Once again, he agreed to meet, but warned me he would not give. "That's OK," I said, grinning at Susan over the phone. "We still want to come."

The second appointment was much like the first, only shorter. This time, his astute observations made it clear he approved of Crystal's work, particularly the way she'd integrated living collections into the college's liberal art curriculum. Once again, Susan asked if he'd consider making a gift. Once again, he said, "No." Susan and I enjoyed the interchange . . . a game by now. Based on the mischievous twinkle in his eyes as he bade us farewell, we thought he'd relished the sparring as well.

Passing a campus meeting room a few months later, I thought I recognized his voice. Slowing down, I overheard Mr. Kravitz bellow, "You don't know what you're doing! You should take a lesson from Val Jones, she *really* knows how to fundraise!"

What the heck? He was telling these sophisticated fundraisers to emulate someone who'd failed. I laughed, somewhat touched that he thought well of me.

I was saddened when he died a few years later. Saddened, then astonished to learn he'd left the arboretum close to $1 million in his will. The moral of the story is this: people need to be heard. You never know when you may open someone's heart, even a crack. I think he appreciated having someone listen, really listen, to him.

In the end, that was all we had to do.

"Forget your perfect offering, there is a crack in everything, that's how the light gets in." Leonard Cohen

Donor Summering in Maine

Attribute: *Attentive*
Saying: *Shut up and listen.*
Action Step: *Listen to your donor, waiting at least three beats after they've finished before you speak.*

Many wealthy Philadelphians flee our steamy summers for the cool crispness of the rocky coast of Maine. I grew up in Maine, and, when visiting my family, sometimes stopped to see a donor who'd become a friend. Amanda was a great gardener with a beautiful house and property by the sea. I called one year, hoping to schedule a visit, and found her distraught. "What's the matter?" I asked.

In her lovely southern accent, and with a great deal of circumlocution, she finally wailed, "Oh, Val, I feel as though I've been taken advantage of!"

"What do you mean? Who was it? What did they do?" I demanded. Slowly, I winkled the story out of her. It took a while, because it wasn't a nice story, and she rarely spoke ill of anyone.

Her husband had died of cancer the year before. She was intensely grateful to the fine medical team who had cared for him with great skill, kindness, and respect. Like her, he was charming and remarkably uncomplaining. The staff had come to love him, further endearing them to her. She'd been thinking of making a $5 million gift to the hospital in his memory, possibly endowing the whole Cancer Center. So, when the hospital's development director, Mr. Daniels, called to ask if he could come to pay his condolences, she happily agreed, tingling in anticipation of surprising him with her colossal gift.

Amanda was disappointed that none of the medical team that she knew and trusted had accompanied him. She toured him through her renowned garden before lunch, but he seemed distracted. She made polite conversation as the meal was served. Southern ladies rarely discuss business over lunch, at least not before the second or third course. So, she was startled when he launched into his spiel right away.

He told her the hospital's fine staff needed funding for a new cancer center. She tried to share her ideas, but he talked right over her. He pulled out architect's sketches (at the table!) and started describing the facilities and equipment, without a mention of the patients. When she tried to ask questions, he glared, silencing her with a firm, "Please don't interrupt." After a few attempts, she gave up. She hid her hurt feelings by looking down at her soup, which seemed to irritate him.

His delicious lunch barely tasted, he completed his presentation by asking, "Don't you think you owe the hospital something for all *we* did for your husband?" She had never met this man before, and was sure *he* hadn't visited, not once in the hundreds of hours she'd sat by her husband's sickbed. She stammered that yes, of course she was grateful, but stopped, shocked, as he slid a pledge card and pen across the table to her.

The form was already filled out . . . indicated she would make a gift of $1 million.

She signed, almost in tears. She'd planned to give $5 million, but he'd robbed her of her delightful vision. She wanted to give those caregivers every bit of space, equipment, and staff they needed. But she also wanted to share her research on the healing gardens they could create, that would freshen the air and lift the spirits, both within the hospital and via intimate walkways around it.

She signed, taking no joy in this cold transaction. He'd smashed her glorious memorial as a bully might kick apart a sandcastle on the nearby beach.

She was heartbroken.

I was speechless, appalled, and deeply grieved that her generous spirit had been so violated. She'd confided in me because she knew I'd understand her loss. We'd happily conspired on successful philanthropic projects, and she knew how fond I was of her husband. I visited her that summer, but we didn't speak of the incident. I admired her garden and we shared a delicious lunch. Afterward, I helped her to a bench by the ocean. Together, we let its crashing waves soothe our spirits.

It's easy to talk over a shy person when you're anxious or excited. And yes, when asking for a gift, you talk about your nonprofit's impact and the resources it needs, but it's as important to *listen* as to speak, to listen deeply and listen well.

Consider this. When did someone last listen to *you* with their whole being? Totally attentive to your every word? When did you last have the luxury of thinking something through aloud without being interrupted? Of discovering your answer in the safe presence of a receptive listener? Besides, as the old saying goes, you learn more with your mouth shut than with it flapping open.

Elizabeth A. Dow, CEO and president of LEADERSHIP Philadelphia, offers the following tips for active listening:

1. Make it your sole agenda to understand the other person.
2. Refrain from judging the person or their words.
3. Do not try to solve their problem or fix them.

4. Meet them where they are.
5. Leave behind everything else going on in your life—be there for them in that moment.

If you can't remember all five, try two simple things. Look into the speaker's eyes and count three beats after they've spoken but before you reply. Our modern Western culture abhors silence, so it may be a bit awkward at first. As you get more comfortable, you'll revel in the spaciousness of such discussions. You will learn more about others and help them discover for themselves what they think.

You may also find you become very popular, because we all want to be heard.

"We need silence to touch souls." Mother Teresa

ACTIVITY: Elevate Your Speech

Perhaps you're a great listener but get tongue-tied when attempting to describe your nonprofit. To overcome, this, many nonprofits ask their boards to memorize an "elevator speech," a succinct summary short enough to convey during an elevator ride. Though helpful for some, memorized speeches tend to sound, well, *memorized.* Fake. Inauthentic. Not in your words. Instead, try elevating your speech by developing a message based on your own experience.

Here's How It Works

You can do this activity solo, but it's more effective and much more fun in a group. You'll stumble at the beginning, which is why you will want to do this in private rather than on your first big solicitation call. By repeating your story over and over, you'll distill it down to an authentic, succinct message that you'll never forget.

Group Version

Select a facilitator to lead this activity and give them a timer. Set up two rows of chairs facing each other. There should be an even number of chairs, with enough room for board members to face each other, and room behind each row for people to move.

Give each person a small notepad and a pen.

1. A's and B's: Tell the first row they are the A's and those facing them that they're the B's.
2. Recall the moment (two minutes):
   a. Ask participants to close their eyes and remember the moment they fell in love with this nonprofit. When did they experience its power? What was it that made them a passionate advocate? If it was a gradual realization, how did it evolve? Ask them if they recall the smell of the place, whether it was hot or cold, dark or light, the texture of something they touched, the sound of someone's voice, clatter of background noise or silence. How did they feel, before, during, and after?
   b. Ask them to jot down the experience.
3. First telling: Side A to Side B, then Side B to Side A (four minutes):
   a. Tell Side A they have two minutes to tell their story to the Side B person facing them. Say, "Go!" and start the timer. Alert them as the clock winds down. "Fifteen seconds left!" "Five seconds . . ." Then "Stop!"
   b. Ask Side B to tell Side A their story in two minutes. Give them the same time warnings.
4. Move and do again in one minute (two minutes):
   a. Move: Tell everyone in Side B to move down one seat, to face a new partner. One B at the end of the row will need to circle round to take the now-vacant place at the beginning of Row B.
   b. Ask Side A to tell their story to their new B partner, only now in one minute.
   c. Ask B's to tell the same story to their new A partner in one minute.
5. Move again and do in thirty seconds (one minute).
6. Move again and do in fifteen seconds (thirty seconds).
7. Share with the group (ten to twenty minutes, depending on size of group.) Facilitate discussion. What was it like? Did they learn anything from others? Give everyone a chance to share.

Solo Version

Get a timer or use this function in your cell phone. Find a private place with a mirror. Go through the activity as above, using your mirror. The solo version's less vivid, so you may want to record and replay it to yourself, to reinforce it.

DO IT YOUR WAY

Sixteen Asking Personalities

PLAY TO YOUR STRENGTHS

"Be yourself. Everybody else is taken."

—Oscar Wilde

Comic book heroes have special powers, and so do you.

Superman has extraordinary strength and can fly. Wonder Woman conquers villains with her lasso of truth and bullet-deflecting bracelets. But they also have their weaknesses. Superman can be subdued by Kryptonite, and Wonder Woman weakened by removing her bracelets.

Playing to your strengths—your special powers—will help you raise more money for your nonprofit and have more fun doing it. You learned your Myers–Briggs personality type at the beginning of this book. In this chapter, you'll find an in-depth description of your asking personality and guidance on how you can best thank, engage, research, cultivate, and ask. You'll explore your likely objections, asking strengths, possible weaknesses, choicest opportunities, the kind of support you may need and what you may want to consider when choosing a board. If you don't have time to read your whole profile, check out the quick tips chart (table 3.1) to learn who and how you should ask, what you should request, your likely strengths, possible weaknesses, and which of the five steps you may prefer.

Table 3.1. Quick tips—asking personality chart

	ISTJ-The Good Steward *Most responsible*	**ISFJ**-The Protector *Most loyal*	**INFJ**-The Counselor *Most reflective*	**INTJ**-The Strategist *Most independent*
Who:	Quiet donors	Current donors	Likely donors	Ask institutional funders
How:	Ask on-site	Ask with a partner	Use active listening	Have a plan
What:	Logical needs	Improvements	Motivational projects	Strategic projects
Strengths:	Careful, honest	Attentive, focused	Guide donors wisely	Quickly grasp shared goals
Cautions:	May overprep, not ask	May not ask at all	May not ask at all	May go your own way
Preferred Steps:	Engage, Thank	Thank, Engage	Ask, Cultivate	Research, Ask

	ISTP-The Craftsman *Most practical*	**ISFP**-The Artist *Most aesthetic*	**INFP**-The Idealist *Most integrity*	**INTP**-The Philosopher *Most conceptual*
Who:	Ask pragmatists	Current donors	You can intuit who to ask	Ask institutional funders first
How:	Show, don't tell	Ask on-site	Express your passion	Help make the case
What:	Concrete projects, here, now	Visually appealing projects	Inspiring projects	Innovative ideas
Strengths:	Ask via vivid experiences	Attuned to donors	Value giver over gift	Adept with complex ideas
Cautions:	Value facts over feelings	Can be overly sensitive	May give up too easily	Can value ideas over people
Preferred Steps:	Research, Engage	Engage, Thank	Ask, Cultivate	Research, Cultivate

ESTP-The Entrepreneur
Most spontaneous
Who: High achievers
How: In person, others taking notes
What: Exciting, big-picture projects
Strengths: Consummate persuader
Cautions: May invent, overpromise
Preferred Steps: Cultivate, Ask

ESTJ-The Guardian
Most driven
Who: Ask leading citizens
How: Convey sound finances
What: Concrete, thoughtful projects
Strengths: Inspire trust
Cautions: Can be defensive, get stuck
Preferred Steps: Cultivate, Engage

ESFP-The Performer
Most generous
Who: Ask new contacts
How: Ask in social situations
What: Ask for new opportunities
Strengths: Warm and enthusiastic
Cautions: Can be overly sensitive
Preferred Steps: Cultivate, Thank

ESFJ-The Provider
Most agreeable
Who: Ask peer donors
How: Seek win-win gifts
What: Delicate situations
Strengths: Prepared, sensitive
Cautions: Conflict adverse
Preferred Steps: Engage, Ask

ENFP-The Catalyst
Most optimistic
Who: Shy and conservative donors
How: Share your vision
What: Outreach needs
Strengths: Emphatic catalyst
Cautions: Need to be liked
Preferred Steps: Cultivate, Ask

ENFJ-The Giver
Most persuasive
Who: Ask big donors
How: Seek win-win gifts
What: Transformative projects
Strengths: Lucid and inspiring
Cautions: Conflict adverse
Preferred Steps: Cultivate, Engage

ENTP-The Visionary
Most inventive
Who: Ask intellectuals
How: Reveal new ideas, findings
What: Conceptual, future projects
Strengths: Can take on challenges
Cautions: Can value ideas over people
Preferred Steps: Research, Ask

ENTJ-The Executive
Most masterful
Who: Decision makers
How: Can take on challenges
What: Lead gifts, possibly as chair
Strengths: Compelling speaker
Cautions: Can talk over, daunt donors
Preferred Steps: Ask, Research

THE ARTIST

Introversion, Sensing, Feeling, Perceiving (ISFP)

ISFP Capsule Personality Description

"Quiet, friendly, sensitive, and kind. Enjoys the present moment, what's going on around them. Likes to have their own space and work within their own time frame. Loyal and committed to their values and to people who are important to them. Dislike disagreements and conflict. Does not force their opinions or values on others."[1]

The Five Steps for ISFPs

1. Thanking: Call up the face of the donor you're thanking, or, if you don't know them, someone dear to you. Write as if addressing them. Follow your instincts. Your sensitivity won't steer you wrong. Thanking may be one of your preferred steps in the fundraising process._
2. Engaging: Engage your donors through beauty and by evoking feelings. Use personal stories that "feel right" to you and leave the statistics to others. Engage just a handful of donors, preferably modest individuals as you may find self-promoters annoying. Ask for a flexible schedule. Engaging may be the step you prefer most in the fundraising process.
3. Researching: You say little but notice a lot about the world and people around you. Use your observant and intuitive nature to identify potential supporters who are "hidden in plain sight," such as the bus-stop parent wearing a Nature Conservancy T-shirt. If you're reluctant to share lists of your friends' names with your nonprofit, talk to your contacts individually. You're a good listener and will discern if your cause interests them.
4. Cultivating: You don't like to force your ideas on others, so issue your invites in writing. If your invitation goes unanswered, don't assume it mean total rejection. After all, how much back-and-forth does it take you to schedule lunch with a friend? Try at least three times. Cultivate through on-site experiences where the focus is on your nonprofit's work, not on you, and where staff can help engage prospects.
5. Asking: Asking may be hard for you, but you are so genuine, thoughtful, and mindful of your donor's situation, you'll have a very high success rate. Since you ask little of others, they may be unusually ready to grant your requests.

ISFP's "Yeah, Buts . . ." Usually include the following: "I'm afraid they'll say 'no.' They won't like me. We'll both be embarrassed. They may feel I'm using our friendship to get money. They may not care about what we're doing. I don't know how, where, or when to ask."

ISFP's Asking Strengths You ask authentically, giving others the space and time to make thoughtful decisions. You pick up on conversational nuances that reveal the donor's interests, to which you'll respond sensitively and accurately. Because you value accord, you will not disagree with, challenge, or try to correct a prospective donor.

ISFP's Possible Weaknesses You can be so protective of prospects you don't ask them at all. Hypersensitive to criticism, you may assume your donor has said no, when they're only asking for more information. Even when they say yes, you may shrink from having them to complete a pledge form. Sadly, this can lead to misunderstanding later.

ISFP's Best Opportunities You should ask current or past donors, but perhaps not close friends or relatives. You're a friendly and sensitive team player and can anchor a more outgoing or analytic asking partner. You're good at building relationships and will perform best asking the same donors year after year.

ISFP's Needs Ask to fundraise for concrete, pragmatic projects. Request examples of how the money will be used, what will happen, and how it will benefit constituents. Ask with a knowledgeable partner. It's important that others value your opinion, but you'll rarely volunteer it. Try to include Q&A time in more formal meetings, so there's a graceful way for you to say what you think.

Personal Considerations for ISFPs It is extremely important for ISFPs to serve on the right board, not only in terms of mission but in terms of values, style, and culture. Try volunteering first. Once you're comfortable with the nonprofit, you can work your way up to the board. Avoid groups that don't feel right. Take your time.

Fun Facts

- ISFPs comprise 8.8 percent of the population, 7.6 percent of men, and 9.9 percent of women.[2]
- Fundraisers: Few ISFPs are drawn to careers in fundraising. In a recent Association of Fundraising Professionals (AFP) survey,[3] 1.5 percent of respondents were ISFPs, only a sixth as many as the 8.8 percent of ISFPs in the general population.

THE PROTECTOR

Introversion, Sensing, Feeling, Judging (ISFJ)

ISFJ Capsule Personality Description

"Quiet, friendly, responsible, and conscientious. Committed and steady in meeting their obligations. Thorough, painstaking and accurate. Loyal, considerate, notice and remember specifics about people who are important to them, concerned with how others feel. Strive to create an orderly and harmonious environment at work and at home."[4]

The Five Steps for ISFJs

1. Thanking: Use your people memory to recall what donors care about. For example, if you heard them wondering whether the residents of your homeless shelter have health care coverage, mention the subject in your note. Recipients will appreciate your attentiveness. Write your notes on picture postcards or over a glass of wine to keep it fun. Thanking may be your most preferred step in the fundraising process.

2. Engaging: Your nonprofit can count on you to engage donors well. Ask to have the system of stewarding gifts explained to you, if there is one, so you can do your bit without getting overwhelmed. Look for opportunities to tell heart-warming stories about your cause. Host brunch for a few volunteers, for example, or send newsletters, highlighting items of interest to each of your donors. Engaging may become one of your favorite steps in the fundraising process.

3. Researching: You are an astute judge of human nature. If asked to research an individual, you will collect relevant, appropriate information. You'll patiently review lists of names, and your observations about the donors under discussion will be accurate. You are discreet and mindful of others' privacy. You will take pride in being able to identify new constituents. Once you start looking, you'll soon be sending your nonprofit a steady stream of potential donors.

4. Cultivating: You do best when prospects come to you, either at your nonprofit or at your home or office. You have a knack for creating gracious, welcoming spaces, and may be happy to host an intimate house party, especially with staff support and if partnered with a co-host who'll pull his or her weight. Your guests will have fun and learn more about your cause.

5. Asking: Practice with the easy steps, thanking and engaging, and ask loyal, regular donors. Once you get comfortable, you may be one of your nonprofit's most productive fundraisers, because you will do it, rather than talking, bragging, planning, or perseverating about it.

ISFJ's "Yeah Buts . . ." Often include the following: "I don't know how, where, or when to ask. I don't want to make them feel awkward or uncomfortable or offend them. They'll feel I'm using them, they won't talk to me anymore, they'll think I'm annoying. They'll say no. If I ask them to give to my cause, they'll ask me to give to theirs."

ISFJ's Asking Strengths You are well liked, trusted, prepared, and are sensitive to donor's interests and needs. You keep the conversation focused on your cause and the donor's interests. You speak from the heart and inspire confidence that donors' gifts will be put to good use. You listen attentively. Donors know you're on their side.

ISFJ's Possible Weaknesses Experiencing, or even anticipating, any kind of resistance, will make you shy away. You may worry about your donor's giving more than they do, and minor setbacks can unsettle you. If unhappy, you may let it build up until you resent peers who don't do their fair share and donors who don't give as much as you hope they will. Your greatest weakness is that you may not ask at all.

ISFJ's Best Opportunities Ask those who have given in the past or very likely donors. You're a great asking partner for almost anyone, providing grounding to more extraverted colleagues and sensitivity to the overly analytical. You will remember and accurately report the conversation, ensuring the donors' wishes are fulfilled.

ISFJ's Needs Ask to solicit with a partner and request research profiles on those you will visit. You might like staff to give you sample questions you can pose to your donor. Bring brochures and other reference materials. You tend to work modestly behind the scenes. Make sure you get your fair share of recognition.

Personal Considerations for ISFJs Join a board only if it really interests you, not from a sense of duty, and make sure the cause is aligned with your personal mission. If you have a hard time saying no, explain that you only serve on one board at a time. Conversely, if you're not happy where you are, you have my permission to leave. Don't volunteer for the most tedious jobs . . . you'll get stuck doing them! And don't undervalue yourself. You'll be an asset anywhere.

Fun Facts

- ISFJ is the most frequently occurring type overall (13.8 percent) and among women (19.4 percent); 8.1 percent of men are ISFJs.[5]
- Fundraisers: ISFJs are underrepresented in development. In a recent Association of Fundraising Professionals (AFP) survey,[6] 8.8 percent of respondents were ISFJs, compared to 13.8 percent of ISFJs found in the general population. This is a shame, as we could use more sensitive, hardworking ISFJs.

THE COUNSELOR

Introversion, iNtuitive, Feeling, Judging (INFJ)

INFJ Capsule Personality Description

"Seek meaning and connection in ideas, relationships, and material possessions. Want to understand what motivates people and are insightful about others. Conscientious and committed to their firm values. Develop a clear vision of how best to serve the common view. Organized and decisive in implementing their vision."[7]

Five Steps for INFJs

1. Thanking: You like things done systematically, and want to know who thanks whom, how, and when. If such a system isn't in place, you may develop it. You may have uncanny insight into others, and so thank well. You are gentle and never want to hurt anyone. You will thank a $10 donor with as much sensitivity as a $10,000 one.
2. Engaging: Choose activities where you function independently, preferably one-on-one or with small groups. Follow your instincts. You may engage donors in original ways, such as inviting them to a press conference or a behind-the-scenes tour. Check with staff to ensure your ideas are appropriate before engaging donors.
3. Researching: When reviewing lists of prospective donors, ask what project needs funding the most, and focus on that priority. Employ your astute understanding to discern what may motivate each person. If you're hesitant to share your friends' names with your nonprofit, make a short list of those most likely to find your cause meaningful.

4. Cultivating: Cultivate others in a setting where they come to you. You love helping people to develop their potential and may enjoy training volunteers. You'll make it fun and satisfying. This is important, as volunteering is often a donor's first point of involvement with your cause. Cultivation may be one of your preferred fundraising steps.

5. Asking: You are an excellent team asker and can anchor a more impulsive colleague. Begin by asking steady, longtime donors. Take your time to prepare, review your donors' bios, develop the best approach, and you'll ask in ways that make your donors very happy. You listen well. You can show donors how to fulfill their desires and how they can change the world by making a gift to your nonprofit. Asking may be your most preferred step in the fundraising process.

INFJ "Yeah Buts . . ." May include: "I don't want to put them in that position. It doesn't feel right. How am I supposed to ask? I don't know what to say. I'm afraid they'll say no, reject me, be offended, or think I'm trying to use them. I'm afraid they won't see how important this is."

INFJ's Asking Strengths When you believe in a cause, you do so 100 percent. Donors sense your commitment and trust your integrity. You are a superb listener, often understanding donors better than they do themselves. You help them give in ways that matter to them. You can grasp complex problems and explain how your nonprofit addresses these issues. You help others come to a decision. You will find it satisfying to secure gifts. A little playfulness from you is delightful. Don't leave your sense of fun behind when asking.

INFJ's Possible Weaknesses Your main weakness is that you may not ask at all. You may be overly protective of your donors/prospects. You may dig in your heels and refuse to ask in ways that don't feel right to you. Because you're so dedicated, you may judge others harshly if they fail to fulfill their responsibilities. You can be perfectionistic, failing to ask because the situation's never quite right.

INFJ's Best Opportunities You are eloquent and visionary, so you can describe the positive impact of new ventures, programming, or buildings. Focus on big-picture, big-impact projects. You should begin with asking, and perhaps always asking those who are already donors. You will also be good at asking quiet folks as you listen well and can draw them out. You won't overwhelm them as more extraverted askers might.

INFJ's Needs Don't weigh yourself down with paperwork or let yourself be pushed to ask in a way that's insensitive. You prefer time and space to process information. If you're assigned certain prospects, ask for time to think it over. You'll do a wonderful job with those you agree to ask.

Personal Considerations for INFJs You'll thrive on the juice you get from charismatic leadership and the chance to work with dynamic, visionary, and optimistic peers. Steer clear of boards rife with power politics and leaders who put others down. You can exhaust yourself, even get sick working for your cause. Remember asking is a team effort and many people are responsible for your nonprofit's success.

Fun Facts

- INFJ is the rarest type in the population overall (1.5 percent), the rarest for men (1.3 percent), and the second rarest among women (1.6 percent).[8]
- Fundraisers: INFJs are exceptional fundraisers. In a recent Association of Fundraising Professionals (AFP) survey,[9] 12.7 percent of respondents were INFJs, compared to only 1.5 percent of INFJs found in the general population. Though the rarest type in the population, this study found there were more fundraising INFJs than any other type of respondent.

THE IDEALIST

Introversion, iNtuitive, Feeling, Perceiving (INFP)

INFP Capsule Personality Description

"Idealistic to their values and to people who are important to them. Want an external life that is congruent with their values. Curious, quick to see possibilities, can be catalysts for implementing ideas. Seek to understand people and help them fulfill their potential. Adaptable, flexible and accepting unless a value is threatened."[10]

The Five Steps for INFPs

1. Thanking: If you're a writer, you can turn an ordinary thank-you note into an eloquent poem or a moving story. If you're artistic, you may create unique stationery about your nonprofit. You may come up with original ways to thank, like recording children as they play or learn a

lesson, having them say thank you, then playing the recording for your delighted and astonished donors.

2. Engaging: Bring your donors to thought-provoking lectures. Share interesting experiences where they can see their dollars at work. If your creative abilities include writing or graphics, volunteer to help with your nonprofit's annual report, newsletters, or e-blasts. You probably have a talent for developing engaging images and captivating stories that make superb social media posts.

3. Researching: Pick one aspect of your nonprofit's work that's particularly important to you and go for it. For example, a zoo board member with a background in education learned that three schools couldn't afford Zoo-on-Wheels. She scoured the news, talked to friends, and made calls until she identified a radio DJ to publicize the need, a list of National Science Teachers Association sponsors, and one wealthy philanthropist.

4. Cultivating: You may enjoy training volunteers or serving as a docent. You have a talent for self-expression and may enjoy serving on your nonprofit's speaker's bureau. If you're bilingual, you might like translating. Challenge yourself to use your linguistic ability to connect your nonprofit to a broader base of supporters. Cultivation may become one of your preferred steps in the fundraising process.

5. Asking: Ask current donors first, preferably those you know. Seek out donors for whom you think giving will be a growth experience. Avoid confrontational or argumentative donors. Tap your passion to give you the courage to ask for what you believe in. Asking may be your most preferred step in the fundraising process.

INFP's "Yeah, Buts . . ." May include: "They won't like me, they'll be mad at me, and/or think I'm using them for money. They'll say no, they'll reject me. I'm not the right person to ask, I don't think I'll ask well. How am I supposed to ask? I don't know what to say. Why do we have to ask at all? They should just give."

INFP's Asking Strengths You can translate complicated concepts into easy to understand images and metaphors. Your belief in your donors makes them want to live up to your good image of them. You're authentic and trustworthy. If donors want to help, you'll find creative ways they can do so, even if they're not wealthy. You care more about the giver than the gift. Donors rarely feel judged by you.

INFP's Possible Weaknesses You won't ask if you equate fundraising with high-pressure sales because you dislike controlling others as much as you loathe being controlled yourself. If you encounter resistance when asking, you may give up, quickly agreeing with the donor that they shouldn't give. Alternately, if a donor withholds support, you may take it personally and become defensive.

INFP's Best Opportunities You are accepting of others and intrigued by offbeat points of view and alternative lifestyles. You are the perfect person to visit that oddball hermit who nobody knows, or the flaky, endearing old lady. Stick to donors at first.

INFP's Needs You are motivated by ideals, so challenges and deadlines are not helpful. Choose a pragmatic asking partner who'll handle the research beforehand and paperwork afterward, freeing you to inspire donors. Avoid conflict-ridden situations, such as asking donors who are friends of a recently fired employee. Never make cold calls. You can doubt yourself, so work with an affirming and supportive partner.

Personal Considerations for INFPs Volunteer before going on a board, perhaps sampling several nonprofits engaged in a cause you care about. Steer clear of nonprofits rife with office politics, conflict, and/or where you are likely to be criticized. When you're on fire, you're unstoppable, which means you can also burn out. Ask a handful of committed donors and try not to overextend yourself.

Fun Facts

- INFPs comprise 4.4 percent of the population, 4.1 percent of men, and 4.6 percent of women.[11]
- Fundraisers: There were about twice as many INFP fundraisers (8.5 percent) as there are INFPs in the general population (4.4 percent), judging by respondents to a recent Association of Fundraising Professionals (AFP) survey.[12]

THE GOOD STEWARD

Introversion, Sensing, Thinking, Judging (ISTJ)

ISTJ Capsule Personality Description

"Quiet, serious, earn success by thoroughness and dependability. Practical, matter-of-fact, realistic, and responsible. Decide logically what should be done and work toward it steadily, regardless of distractions. Take pleasure in making everything orderly and organized—their work, their home, their life. Value traditions and loyalty."[13]

The Five Steps for ISTJs

1. Thanking: You find writing thank-you notes satisfying, doing so promptly and specifically. You may say something like, "Thanks for your pledge of $30,000 toward the animal hospital. We've received your first payment of $10,000, and will send reminders for your next two payments." Donors will appreciate your attention to detail . . . after all, they're giving a lot of money! Thanking may become one of your favorite steps in the fundraising process.

2. Engaging: Your written reports are concise and to the point. In person, you enjoy sharing your nonprofit with donors, leading a behind-the-scenes tour, for example, or demonstrating the advantages of a new facility. You'll be more comfortable on your home turf. You're observant and a good listener. Your insights will help your nonprofit engage donors more deeply. Engaging may be your best fundraising step.

3. Researching: You're excellent at identifying and qualifying potential donors and may bring many contacts to the table. Your approach to prospect research is logical, methodical, and fruitful, in part because you're decisive. You'll skip the long shots in favor of wealthy prospects with clear reasons for giving. Conscientious, you can review prospects either in a group or on your own.

4. Cultivating: Cultivate potential donors on-site, where they can come to your nonprofit, rather than you going to them. You'll enjoy watching them experience it themselves. Who needs to talk when they can participate in a historic reenactment or try the new slide with kids at the park? At social events, you may prefer being useful to chatting up strangers. Volunteer to staff the check-in table or to manage auction items.

5. Asking: You do best asking long-term, regular donors, with whom you can build relationships over time. Solicit those who've already demonstrated support in other ways (e.g., by attending events or volunteering). You'll be more comfortable leading by example, making your own gift before asking others to donate.

ISTJ's "Yeah, Buts . . ." May include the following: "I'm afraid they'll say no, that they won't like me, or think I'm using them to get their money.

How do we know they'll give at all? What if we're not organized enough or they ask me something I don't know? I can't ask if I don't know how much the project will cost and when it will be done. If this doesn't make sense for them, I'm not doing it."

ISTJ's Asking Strengths   You will notice details in what the donor says and how they respond to the project you're proposing. You are superbly consistent, staying on script and playing your correct role in any team solicitation. You won't go off on tangents and will ensure everyone is agreed on next steps before concluding your visit. You are a person of integrity. Donors will appreciate your honesty and trust you with their money.

ISTJ's Possible Weaknesses   You'll resist asking if you see fundraising as a sign of weakness. You may spend too much time preparing. You may judge prospects negatively if they don't agree with your position, rather than accepting them as they are and seeking common ground. You are not overtly emotional and may miss some cues from donors who respond more to feeling than to facts.

ISTJ's Best Opportunities   You'll succeed with existing donors, particularly those you know through your place of worship, business, or civic association. You're very good at asking the elderly, listening patiently and respectfully, and enjoying their company. Private, reserved donors will welcome your quiet approach. In the long run, you may succeed with them where a flamboyantly extraverted peer would fail.

ISTJ's Needs   Ask for donor profiles, a case statement, and related materials, like an FAQ with impact measures. This will help you explain how your nonprofit differs from those with similar missions. You'll want to understand how your assignment fits into the overall fundraising campaign. Ask for regular progress reports so you know where you stand and that everyone else is pulling their weight.

Personal Considerations for ISTJs   Once you've joined a board, you'll likely serve a long time, so choose carefully. Check out the finances in advance and don't let others dump their work on you. You'll want well-run, productive board meetings, with agendas distributed in advance and minutes afterward. If your life is already full of duties and responsibilities, pick a nonprofit that'll be fun for you.

Fun Facts

- ISTJ is the third most common (11.5 percent) type in the population and the most common among men (16.4 percent). Only 6.9 percent of women are ISTJs.[14]

- Fundraisers: There are about half as many ISTJs in fundraising as in the population. In a recent Association of Fundraising Professionals (AFP) survey,[15] 6.3 percent of respondents were ISTJs, compared to 11.5 percent of ISTJs in the general population.

THE STRATEGIST

Introversion, iNtuitive, Thinking, Judging (INTJ)

INTJ Capsule Personality Description

"Have original minds and great drive for implementing their ideas and achieving their goals. Quickly see patterns in external events and develop long-range explanatory perspectives. When committed, organize a job and carry it through. Skeptical and independent, have high standards of competence and performance—for themselves and others."[16]

The Five Steps for INTJs

1. Thanking: In addition to thanking your donors, tell them how their gift fits into the big picture, helping your nonprofit to achieve its strategic goals. You may also want to remind them that there is still much to do, and list some of the exciting challenges your cause plans to tackle in the future.
2. Engaging: Engage donors through ideas, such as inviting them to join you in an after-show discussion of a new play or involving them in strategic planning. Tell them the quantifiable difference their gift has made. Everything you do, you do well, and you may devise entirely new engagement strategies, such as sending tulip bulbs to garden donors in the fall, timed to arrive a few weeks before your annual appeal.
3. Researching: You will quickly determine the most effective way you can help identify and research prospective donors for your nonprofit. Your approach to prospect research sessions will likely be intellectual rather than social/emotional. Challenge yourself to find donors interested in your most strategically important initiatives. Research may be your best step in the fundraising process.
4. Cultivating: Focus your cultivation efforts with laser-like intensity on your highest priority prospects. Tailor your approaches to fit each donor. Some might enjoy a lively discussion over lunch with your CEO:

others may prefer the anonymity of watching a show. Before social events, make a list of those you intend to meet. Galas will be more fun if you think of them as a chessboard where kings and queens connect to advance your cause.

5. Asking: Ask for funding to underwrite the projects that interest you most, probably long-range planning or innovative strategies. Practice with current donors until you're comfortable. The amount matters less to you than the donor's willingness to support your nonprofit's strategy. Solicit smart, strategic thinkers, avoiding self-promoters and overly conservative thinkers. Asking may be one of your best fundraising steps.

INTJ's "Yeah, Buts . . ."   May include the following: "Why should they give? Am I the right person to ask? Can they give this much? I don't want to risk failing, being told no, or being rejected. What if they don't understand why this is so important? Why are we fundraising at all? Can't we accomplish what we need via earned revenue?"

INTJ's Asking Strengths   Set yourself a fundraising goal. Once you do, you'll achieve it. You'll quickly see how your nonprofit's needs align with your donor's goals. You're well prepared yet flexible, responding to new ideas as they unfold, rarely slowed by small talk or distracted by tangents. You listen well and end meetings with clear next steps. You have no problem sharing the credit with others when you succeed.

INTJ's Possible Weaknesses   You can be impatient with those who insist your nonprofit should do things as they've always been done. You may refuse to ask if overdirected or told to do so in a way that doesn't make sense. You can be overconfident, causing you to miss emotional cues or override issues that are important to you donor. You disdain ditherers and self-promoters.

INTJ's Best Opportunities   You'll seize opportunities others may not even notice, asking each donor to support that part of the plan that suits them best. You will excel at soliciting corporations, foundations, and government agencies. You will do well with reserved donors, especially planners who like to proceed in a logical manner, such as donors with backgrounds in IT, builders, engineers, and/or some corporate leaders.

INTJ's Needs   You ask best as a highly effective, independent operative, perhaps reporting directly to the CEO and well supported by staff. You need accurate information in the format you prefer, including details on the donors you'll be visiting. Ask to see your nonprofit's fundraising and strategic plans. Demand prompt follow-up by your nonprofit, as you'll hate looking incompetent to anyone, especially big donors.

Personal Considerations for INTJs Audit a board meeting before joining to ensure it is well run. Since most boards are made up of accomplished individuals working together to achieve a shared purpose, you may find board service very satisfying. Your integrity, accomplishments, confidence, and informed decision-making will be valuable to any board. Take your time and choose strategically.

Fun Facts

- INTJs are the third rarest type in the population (2.1 percent).[17]
- Fundraisers: A recent survey of Association of Fundraising Professionals (AFP)[18] members found there were more than twice as many INTJ fundraisers (5.7 percent) as there are INTJs in the general population (2.1 percent).

THE PHILOSOPHER

Introversion, iNtuitive, Thinking, Perceiving (INTP)

INTP Capsule Personality Description

"Seek to develop logical explanations for everything that matters to them. Theoretical and abstract, interested more in ideas than in social interactions. Quiet, contained, flexible, and adaptable. Have unusual ability to focus in depth to solve problems in their area of interest. Skeptical, sometimes critical, always analytical."[19]

The Five Steps for INTPs

1. Thanking: Routine social obligations are not your forte. Since you can be the "absent-minded professor," and sometimes procrastinate, let your nonprofit handle your acknowledgments. You can provide the icing on the cake. For example, if you read an article that pertains to an issue of interest to your donor, forward it on, reminding them of the connection and thanking them for their support.
2. Engaging: Engage donors through ideas, such as inviting them to an after-show discussion of a play or to participate in strategic planning.

If you're supposed to send them progress reports, get a sample, and do so via email. Plan to carbon copy your nonprofit on your email correspondence so that they can follow up (and remind you if you forget!)

3. Researching: If you're good at data management/system design, challenge yourself to devise a simple, free way to help your nonprofit identify wealthy constituents. You may be a surprisingly shrewd judge of human character because you are unimpressed by possessions, charisma, or social standing. You see what is, not what people want you to see. Research may be your most preferred step in the fundraising process.

4. Cultivating: Use the Cultivation Activity chart in chapter 2 to identify one or two cultivation opportunities you can enjoy with intimate groups. If you like puzzles and wordplay, perhaps you could invent ways your nonprofit can engage new supporters online, such as environmentally themed crossword puzzles. If you're thinking, "I can come up with something cleverer than that," I challenge you to do so! Approached this way, you may find cultivation becomes one of your preferred fundraising steps.

5. Asking: Pick the newest idea/theory/approach your nonprofit needs funded and help make the case to relevant government agencies, foundations, and/or corporations. You will be particularly effective when helping to develop grants proposals if you're a content expert who is knowledgeable about the initiative to be funded.

INTP's "Yeah, Buts . . ." May include: "I don't know if they have money. What if they say no? I don't want to fail. I don't want to be embarrassed. We need more data to be sure they'll give. This whole plan doesn't make sense to me; let's redesign it before we ask for funding. I have more important things to do. Isn't there an easier way to do this?"

INTP's Asking Strengths You are excited by new ideas, quickly grasp complex theories, and can pitch innovative projects. You convey information with admirable precision so that the donor knows exactly what their gift will accomplish. You're thoughtful and to the point. Unfazed by offbeat attire or unusual lifestyle choices, you'll successfully solicit eccentrics, providing they are logical eccentrics.

INTP's Possible Weaknesses You don't like to lead or control people and will balk if you think that's what you're doing when fundraising. You may go off on interesting tangents. You may correct a donor if they make errors of language or grammar. You may miss or avoid emotional clues. You may fear failure and worry that there's always one more piece of data you need before you can ask. This can be paralyzing.

INTP's Best Opportunities   Help solicit government agencies or large foundations, in person and possibly in developing grant proposals. Most grantswriters hate making logic models, but you'll create elegant and precise ones. A brilliant devil's advocate, you'll find and correct any proposal's weaknesses. If you are an academic, your credentials may help secure an audience with funders. You may also succeed soliciting peers with whom you can explore exciting new ideas.

INTP's Needs   Ask your nonprofit to provide logistical support and reminders for your tasks and appointments. Ask if you can work behind the scenes to improve systems/grantswriting. Review material before soliciting and make any corrections you deem necessary. Have an asking partner handle logistics before visits and follow up after. You may not want them along, but you probably need them.

Personal Considerations for INTPs   The ideal board for you is one that generates ideas and solutions, not a hands-on working board. Pick a nonprofit populated by creative, open-minded leaders. If invited to a board, ask your recruiters why they want you and what role they expect you to play. You'll want a board that articulates its needs and that proceeds rationally and strategically.

Fun Facts

- INTPs make up 3.3 percent of the population, 4.8 percent of men, and 1.8 percent of women, making it the third rarest MBTI type among women.[20]
- Fundraisers: In a recent Association of Fundraising Professionals (AFP) survey,[21] 1.8 percent of respondents were INTPs, compared to 3.3 percent of INTPs in the general population, meaning INTPs are slightly underrepresented in fundraising.

THE CRAFTSMAN

Introversion, Sensing, Thinking, Perceiving (ISTP)

ISTP Capsule Personality Description

"Tolerant and flexible, quiet observers until a problem appears, then act quickly to find workable solutions. Analyze what makes things work and readily get through large amounts of data to isolate the core of practical problems. Interested in cause and effect, organize facts using logical principles, value efficiency."[22]

The Five Steps for ISTPs

1. Thanking: You are the most pragmatic of all types, but easily bored, so make thanking interesting. Good with your hands, you might like creating your own stationery, or carving little gifts. Focus on thanking donors for the impact they've made. Ask your nonprofit to give you specific, concrete examples, such as, "Your $100 sheltered a family of three overnight during subzero weather."
2. Engaging: You are loyal to and appreciative of donors; you see as your comrades in arms, fighting together for a noble cause. You may prefer active engagement, such as leading a behind-the-scenes tour or birding trip at dawn. You're not keen on committees but can recruit donors to join you in ad hoc groups assembled to achieve a specific purpose. Engaging may be a preferred fundraising step.
3. Researching: You can help identify prospects if the process is logical and efficient, such as reviewing lists of your professional colleagues or college classmates, and if lists are prioritized, such as by giving capacity. Though reserved, you are observant of others and may contribute insightful comments during prospect rating sessions. If you're of a technical bent, you may help structure your nonprofit's database to capture and leverage prospecting data. Research may be your best step in the asking process.
4. Cultivating: Cultivate via hands-on activities, such as demonstrating the difference between a gush of clean, potable water and the slow flow of polluted water, or by rappelling down a cliff or white-water rafting. Just don't lose your prospective donors along the way!
5. Asking: Solicit straight shooters, like-minded individuals who get things done without a lot of fuss. Discover what your nonprofit needs (facilities, equipment, etc.), and fundraise for that. After you've had some practice with easy, regular donors, you can ask for large gifts. Your goal, funds to solve a problem, is more important to you than your own ego, and you're hard to intimidate.

ISTP's "Yeah, Buts . . ." May include the following: "I'm afraid I won't be good at it; they'll turn me down. I'm not a schmoozer. What if they think I'm just there for the money? I don't want to embarrass myself.

They shouldn't have to be asked . . . they should just give. I don't know how fundraising works. I don't know how to do it."

ISTP's Asking Strengths You prefer action to conversation. Try leading donors down to a subbasement so that they can see the dying furnace for themselves. Haul them up to the attic when it's raining to illustrate the need for a new roof. Your penchant for showing, rather than telling, donors makes you an unusual but extraordinarily effective fundraiser.

You can seize the moment, eschewing scripts to ask in your own direct way. Eminently logical, you will not be deterred by frivolous or irrelevant objections. When you're on a mission and are convinced you're right, you are unstoppable.

ISTP's Possible Weaknesses If the request doesn't make sense to you, you may refuse to ask. You can lose patience with indecisive donors and may be uncomfortable with overt displays of emotion. You may describe tangible benefits rather than addressing the feelings that motivate most gifts. You can be stubborn when you think a donor's in the wrong and when you're right, which, let's face it, you usually are.

ISTP's Best Opportunities You'll be good asking down-to-earth, outdoors, and/or pragmatic donors. Solicit the strong, silent types, those who listen more than they talk, and act more than they listen. Developers, engineers, and manufacturers may be good prospects for you. Focus on accomplished yet unpretentious donors, as you've little patience for self-aggrandizement.

ISTP's Needs Tell your nonprofit you prefer asking in the field rather than in an office or over lunch. Take a handful of donors you can pursue in your own way and in your own time. You're great in a crisis if a donor must be asked right now to fund something urgent.

Personal Considerations for ISTPs You may prefer a board that meets quarterly rather than monthly, or serving on an advisory board, where you're tapped on an as-needed basis for your special expertise and strengths. You need time alone, so don't overbook yourself with board commitments.

Fun Facts

- ISTPs make up 5.4 percent of the population, only 2.4 percent of women, but 8.5 percent of men, making it the third most frequently occurring type among men.[23]
- Fundraisers: In a recent Association of Fundraising Professionals (AFP) survey,[24] 0.9 percent of respondents were ISTPs, compared to 5.4 percent of ISTPs in the population at large, or only one-sixth as many fundraisers.

THE GIVER

Extraversion, iNtuitive, Feeling, Judging (ENFJ)

ENFJ Capsule Personality Description

"Warm, empathetic, responsive, and responsible. Highly attuned to the emotions, needs, and motivations of others. Find potential in everyone, want to help others fulfill their potential. May act as catalysts for individual and group growth. Loyal, responsive to praise and criticism. Sociable, facilitate others in a group, and provide inspiring leadership."[25]

The Five Steps for ENFJs

1. Thanking: You write warm, sensitive, and personal thank-you notes. You may enjoy creating or choosing unique cards and gifts for donors. Feel free to express the feelings donations evoke in you: gratitude, surprise, delight, curiosity, humility. You're the kind of board member who'll get to know staff and ensure they're thanked as well.

2. Engaging: You are a superb storyteller. Try connecting each donor to the story and experience that's right for them. You'll take vicarious pleasure as your donors explore your nonprofit and get to know it better. Use the Cultivation Activity Chart from chapter 2 to bring your donors closer to your mission and vision. Engaging may be one of your preferred steps in the fundraising process.

3. Researching: Your quick understanding of your nonprofit's programs and projects will help you identify the right prospects for your cause. Use your talent for figuring out what makes each prospect tick. A strong writer, you'll be good at creating prospect/donor profiles. If you have a broad network, you may find you're only one to two degrees of separation from the people you hope to reach.

4. Cultivating: Charismatic, energetic, and social, you are good at and enjoy cultivation. You like helping to grow institutional relationships and do it well, able to speak to almost anyone. You're also very loyal. You'll remember those you first attracted to your cause, even if it was decades ago. Cultivation may be the step you prefer most in the fundraising process.

5. Asking: You ask for the right amount, in the right way, and at the right time, ensuring everyone is happy. Begin by asking current donors who are as serious and committed to the cause as you are. Naturally

donor-centric, you can ask almost any donor, providing the request is logical and strategic.

ENFJ's "Yeah, Buts . . ." Your fears may include, "They won't like me; I don't want to make them uncomfortable or make them mad at me; I don't want to ask them to give if they don't want to; I don't know if they can afford it; I'm not sure what to say."

ENFJ's Asking Strengths You lead by example and are often the first to donate when a need arises. You ask authentically and thoughtfully. Your optimism is contagious, inspiring donors to live up to your high expectations of them. You are a superb communicator, who can ask well in writing, one-on-one, or by addressing a large audience. You may be most energized addressing a group.

ENFJ's Possible Weaknesses You may be so protective of donors that you refrain from asking if there's even a chance it might distress them. You sometimes shy from conflict. Because you believe the best of everyone, nonresponsive donors can unduly discourage you. Like the Blues Brothers, you're "on a mission from God," and can become impatient if thwarted. You may overcommit and/or procrastinate.

ENFJ's Best Opportunities Energetic, positive, and eager, you can ask lots of people. You bond quickly and excel at persuading others to your ideas, so you can ask nondonors to become donors, lapsed donors to return to the fold, and encourage large donors to give more.

ENFJ's Needs You need to know that this is the right ask for your donor. Ask for their full bio, their career, family, place in the community, hobbies, and so forth. You need to be thanked and will be delighted when your efforts are acknowledged. It will also give you satisfaction to review a list of awards and distinctions your nonprofit has won, so ask for a "brag sheet."

Personal Considerations for ENFJs You are acutely aware of others' emotions, so empathetic that you channel the feelings of those around you. Choose a nonprofit with an encouraging, cooperative, and respectful culture. You can neglect your own needs while caring for others. Be gentle with yourself while you're saving the world.

Fun Facts

- ENFJs make up 2.5 percent of the population; 3.3 percent of women, and 1.6 percent of men, making it the second rarest type among men.[26]
- Fundraisers: A recent Association of Fundraising Professionals (AFP) survey[27] found that there were four times as many ENFJ fundraising

respondents (10 percent) as the percentage of ENFJs occurring in the population (2.5 percent).

THE CATALYST

Extraversion, iNtuitive, Feeling, Perceiving (ENFP)

ENFP Capsule Personality Description

"Warmly enthusiastic and imaginative. See life as full of possibilities. Make connections between events and information very quickly and confidently proceed based on the patterns they see. Want a lot of affirmation from others and readily give appreciation and support. Spontaneous and flexible, often rely on their ability to improvise and on their verbal fluency."[28]

The Five Steps for ENFPs

1. Thanking: You like thanking others as much as being thanked yourself . . . which is a lot. Make sure your donors get an official thank-you from your nonprofit. Because if there's a long list of donors, you may forget to thank them or procrastinate doing so. When you do write, your thanks are charming and heartfelt. Try calling donors as part of a thank-a-thon or writing them in a social setting, at a board meeting, or over a glass of wine.

2. Engaging: Start by engaging just a handful of donors, as you sometimes start more than you finish. You'll discover just the right way to engage each donor, whether it's a hands-on project or lunching with the CEO, and you'll make it fun. Though a good team player, you prefer to be spontaneous and independent. Ask what's expected of you so that you can play your role with flair.

3. Researching: You have a wide circle of friends from a variety of backgrounds, most of whom you're willing to introduce to your cause. You're good at prospect research sessions because you're curious about people, their motivations, and their interests. Your nonprofit could hold prospecting sessions every month for a year, and you'd come up with new names, connections, and strategies every time.

4. Cultivating: You are extremely empathic, can connect with almost anyone, and enjoy getting to know people. Affectionate and popular,

you love being the life of the party and tend to sweep others up in the fun. You'll ensure no wallflower's left behind, that friends and strangers alike have a good time, basking in the glow of your buoyant spirit. Cultivation may be one of your most preferred steps in the fundraising process.

5. Asking: Tackle a few high-dollar prospects and ask for transformative gifts. Do your homework, but don't let naysayers, if there are any, hold you back. If you want to go out and ask, do it. You may become your nonprofit's most successful fundraiser ever. Asking may be your best step in the fundraising process.

ENFP's "Yeah, Buts . . ." May include: "If I ask they won't like me anymore. I'm afraid they'll ask me questions I can't answer. I don't know how to ask. I don't know what to say. I'm afraid I may not ask for the right amount. What if I ask for too little?"

ENFP's Asking Strengths You improvise superbly, quickly grasping and adjusting to any surprises you encounter. You'll say just the right thing to each donor, regardless of social status or background. You can steer a conversation naturally toward your chosen subject. You enjoy encouraging others to join you in making the world a better place. You can convey the big picture and get funds for new programs and facilities.

ENFP's Possible Weaknesses Your greatest weakness is that you may not ask because of your need to be liked and fear of conflict. You may rely too heavily on your ability to wing it, failing to prepare or leaving it to the last moment. As a result, you may inadvertently misrepresent your nonprofit or its programs. If, in your enthusiasm, you take on too many prospects, you may get overwhelmed and not ask anyone.

ENFP's Best Opportunities You can solicit almost anyone but have a special gift for drawing people out of their shells. You'll go to great lengths and be surprisingly persistent in your desire to connect with reserved donors. You may have a zany charm that, interestingly, endears you to stodgy types. In short, you can ask people who are shy or set in their ways, and so difficult for others to ask.

ENFP's Needs You'll function best with strong staff support and an asking partner who is good with data and logistics. Though extraverted, you need time alone to regroup and can be vulnerable to social fatigue. You need to be thanked. If not, you may feel you've poured out your soul only to be neglected. Don't be shy about suggesting that committee members (like you), as well as donors, deserve applause.

Personal Considerations for ENFPs   Get to know your nonprofit before you give yourself wholeheartedly to it. You'll want to operate independently while staying connected enough so you don't get a reputation for being a rogue board member. You can overgive, both personally and financially. Pace yourself so you don't neglect your health and possibly your wealth.

Fun Facts

- ENFPs are 8.1 percent of the population, 6.4 percent of men, and nearly a tenth (9.7 percent) of women.[29]
- Fundraisers: In a recent Association of Fundraising Professionals (AFP) survey, 11.5 percent of respondents were ENFPs, compared to 8.1 percent in the general population, almost 50 percent more in development than one might expect.[30]

THE PERFORMER

Extraversion, Sensing, Feeling, Perceiving (ESFP)

ESFP Capsule Personality Description

"Outgoing, friendly, and accepting. Exuberant lovers of life, people and material comforts. Enjoy working with others to make things happen. Bring common sense and a realistic approach to their work and make work fun. Flexible and spontaneous, adapt readily to new people and environments. Learn best by trying a new skill with other people."[31]

The Five Steps for ESFPs

1. Thanking: You are warm, friendly, and highly observant of people, so you'll thank well in writing, but even better in person or calling as part of a thank-a-thon. You may choose beautifully designed stationery. You can be scattered or procrastinate, so have your nonprofit send the official thanks in case you leave your notes unwritten too long. Thanking may be one of your preferred steps in the fundraising process.
2. Engaging: Engage donors in ways that put you in the limelight, such as giving talks or hosting receptions. You're great at seizing opportunities as they arise, conveying the exciting immediacy of a donor's

impact. Let someone help you engage your annual donors so that you don't tire of them. Otherwise, they may feel dazzled when you ask, then dropped.

3. Researching: You'll enjoy the social aspect of prospect research sessions as you have a wide and varied circle of contacts. You often know someone who knows someone and will ask your friends to introduce them to your cause. Include staff in your social media network so that they can keep up with your ever-expanding circle.

4. Cultivating: Your spontaneity and *joie de vivre* mean you excel at cultivating many people, your own contacts, and those of your more reserved peers. You have the strongest aesthetic sense of any MBTI type, and can decorate with great flair. You encourage and inspire others to join your cause, energize them to act, and make it fun to do so. Cultivation may be your best step in the fundraising process.

5. Asking: Ask donors, not prospects, for exciting, immediate, and tangible projects. You'll fundraise well for a crisis. Generous yourself, you expect the same of others. Embrace asking as a skill to learn and you'll enjoy the process, especially the applause, attention, and gratitude you'll receive when you bring home a whopping big gift!

ESFP's "Yeah, Buts . . ."   May include the following: "What if they don't like me, or get angry because I asked them for money? What if they think I'm using them? I'm afraid they'll want lots of facts and figures. They may not 'get it.' I may ask for too little!"

ESFP's Asking Strengths   Your enthusiasm, vitality, and idealism are contagious, inspiring others to do their best. If questioned, you can think on your feet or you may respond with an "I don't know, let's find out!" You have great social antenna will sense if your donor's upset about something, and likely offer to help, which is endearing. You are warm, friendly, and very well liked.

ESFP's Possible Weaknesses   You need approval, so if you think people will dislike you for asking, you'll never do it. You hate conflict, especially if you feel criticized or misunderstood. You can take things too personally, overreact, or generalize. Even a gentle decision not to give may hurt your feelings. Ask with a partner who can keep the conversation on track, get the forms signed, and follow up as needed.

ESFP's Best Opportunities   You can and will ask friends as well as those new to your nonprofit. You like big ideas and can ask for big dollars. You're great at asking for new programs and initiatives that are needed here and now, rather than those in the far future. Focus on a few prospects at a time.

ESFP's Needs   Prep with a few key points and practice aloud. In speaking to yourself, you'll learn what you want to say and how to say it. Role plays will be a fun way for you to prep and learn. You're a great storyteller but need to experience things for yourself with all five senses and your emotions. Ask staff for hands-on opportunities to get to know your nonprofit's programs.

Personal Considerations for ESFPs   Ask what's expected of you financially before you join a board. Otherwise, you may give more than you can afford. Take time to find a cause you really care about; it will help you stay the course. If you feel criticized, experience conflict, or feel underappreciated, you may pack up your marbles and leave. Don't overcommit, as you may exhaust yourself trying to keep all your promises.

Fun Facts

- ESFPs make up 8.5 percent of the population, 6.9 percent of men, and 10.1 percent of women, making it the third most common type for women.[32]
- Fundraisers: ESFPs may love people but are not drawn to development careers. A recent Association of Fundraising Professionals (AFP) survey[33] found that 1.5 percent of respondents were ESFPs, only about a sixth of the 8.5 percent of ESFPs in the population.

THE PROVIDER

Extraversion, Sensing, Feeling, Judging (ESFJ)

ESFJ Capsule Personality Description

"Warmhearted, conscientious, and cooperative. Want harmony in their environment, work with determination to establish it. Like to work with others to complete tasks accurately and on time. Loyal, follow through even in small matters. Notice what others need in their day-to-day lives and try to provide it. Want to be appreciated for who they are and what they contribute."[34]

The Five Steps for ESFJs

1. Thanking: You can be counted on to thank donors in person as well as in writing. You'll remember and comment on the impact they've made. Make sure public acknowledgments, like donor plaques and donor reports, are fair and inclusive. Thank donors at parties and other social occasions.

2. Engaging: You'll dependably update donors. They'll be flattered by your interest and the way you remember them from year to year. Your loyalty extends to your nonprofit. You'll likely remain on the board for years and be around to engage your donors faithfully and consistently. Engaging may be your best fundraising step.

3. Researching: You are social enough to have a wide circle of friends yet dedicated and detail oriented enough to review lots of names. You like to gather specific relevant information about others. Your super social intelligence enables you to make quick connections. You probably "know the guy" who can snag the introduction you seek.

4. Cultivating: You'll excel at hosting, as well as participating in events for your nonprofit. You'll ensure things go smoothly by tending to a hundred small tasks. People like to be around you as you have a gift for making them feel good about themselves.

5. Asking: Start by asking existing donors. You'll succeed right off the bat. Once comfortable, ask donors who give as much as you do or more. This will place you in social circles you'll enjoy, and you'll raise more money. Fundraising is one of the recommended careers for ES-FJs, so you may be a natural. Asking is one of your best steps in the fundraising process.

ESFJ's "Yeah, Buts . . ."   May include the following: "They won't like me. I don't want to put them in an awkward or uncomfortable position. I'm afraid they'll say no. They'll reject me. They won't want to see me anymore. I'm afraid they'll think I'm using our friendship to get money from them. They'll think I'm bad or thoughtless."

ESFJ's Asking Strengths   You see the best in donors and are good at bringing it out. You'll prep for your meeting, making sure you cover your key points and you will ask. You naturally pick up on emotional clues, responding, and adapting to the mood of those around you. You love win-win situations and will work hard to ensure giving satisfies and pleases your donors. You'll rarely leave without a decision or at least a next step. You'll do whatever it takes to get the job done, including organizing others to ask.

ESFJ's Possible Weaknesses   If you fear fundraising will make you unlikeable, damage your friendships, or make people mad at you, you'll never ask. You can be overly sensitive and take real or perceived rejection personally. Start with well-thanked and engaged donors so you don't have to face a no.

ESFJ's Best Opportunities   You know charity begins at home, and you lead by example, giving generously. You believe everyone should do their part and may be good at chairing the board campaign. You will ask warmly and well but may prefer not to ask those closest to you. You're sensitive to rejection, and a turn-down from a loved one could be devastating.

ESFJ's Needs   Ask nonprofit staff to explain how and when donors are asked, who asks them, why, and for how much. Once the structure and expectations are clear, you'll do a great job. You need to work with equally committed peers and may be annoyed by those who don't pull their weight. You need to be thanked.

Personal Considerations for ESFJs   You're in it for the long haul, so choose your nonprofit carefully. Volunteer first, and steer clear of conflict-ridden boards and/or those who don't value your work. If you give them the shirt off your back and aren't thanked, go elsewhere. You are well liked, organized, and respected. Lots of nonprofits will be happy to have you on their board.

Fun Facts

- ESFJ is the second most frequently occurring type (12.3 percent) in the population and among women (16.9 percent); 7.5 percent of men are ESFJs.[35]
- Fundraisers: Almost a tenth of fundraisers are ESFJs (9.7 percent) according to a recent Association of Fundraising Professionals (AFP) survey,[36] though this is fewer than the 12.3 percent of ESFJs in the general population.

THE EXECUTIVE

Extraversion, iNtuitive, Thinking, Judging (ENTJ)

ENTJ Capsule Personality Description

"Frank, decisive, assumes leadership readily, quickly sees illogical and inefficient policies and procedures, develops and implements comprehensive systems to solve organizational problems. Enjoys long-term planning and goal-setting. Usually well-informed, well-read, enjoys expanding their knowledge and passing it on to others. Forceful in presenting their ideas."[37]

The Five Steps for ENTJs

1. Thanking: You see thanking as an appropriate part of the asking process and, once it becomes a habit, you'll thank regularly and well. Include a piece of information relevant to each of the donors you thank. Make sure your nonprofit notifies you when your donors give and acknowledges their contributions promptly.
2. Engaging: You value accountability, so you're good at engaging and will tell donors the impact their gift has made. A natural leader, you deepen donor connections by getting them involved, urging them to volunteer or join a committee.
3. Researching: You collect people as others collect stamps. You excel at research but can get lost in it. Let staff do the online research and use your extensive network to get the personal angle on prospective donors. In prospect rating sessions, you'll see patterns and make connections others would miss. Research may be one of your preferred steps in the fundraising process.
4. Cultivating: Cultivate donors or funders when there's a logical connection between their interests or guidelines and your nonprofit's mission, such as their history of contributing to similar causes. You are happy to meet new people and eloquent on behalf of your cause. You like to set and achieve goals, so ask for a list of three to four people to cultivate when you attend an event.
5. Asking: You can be an exceptional fundraiser, not only in your ability to ask, but to do so intelligently and strategically, especially if there's a pressing need and a clear deadline. You'll be even more successful in the company of other high-performing, competitive types. Asking may be your best step in the fundraising process.

ENTJ's "Yeah, Buts . . ." May sound like this: "I'm afraid they'll think I'm using our friendship to get their money. They won't like me anymore. I'll be rejected, I'll fail. Why me? Why them? Why now? What's the asking strategy?"

ENTJ's Asking Strengths You're articulate, clear, and compelling when making your case. You quickly grasp and convey essential points (as well as the fascinating details). You can explain long-range, strategic plans. Forceful and decisive, you guide donors through the conversation while keeping your eyes on the prize. You can lead a capital campaign or chair the fundraising committee of the board.

ENTJ's Possible Weaknesses   You hate asking for help for yourself. If you equate asking with weakness or think it will compromise your friendships or integrity in any way, you won't do it. You may talk more than you listen and can intimidate shy or less analytical prospects. You may provide more info than needed. You may correct donors you disagree with and sometimes rush to closure.

ENTJ's Best Opportunities   You can and will ask for big gifts, though not without a rationale. You won't hesitate to ask if you're convinced a gift makes sense, that it will meet a funder's objectives or fulfill a donor's deep desires. You'll do a good job with corporations, foundations, and government agencies as well as individual donors.

ENTJ's Needs   You need a well-organized, highly competent, and possibly competitive team that meets regularly to achieve its goal. Ask to see the fundraising plan and materials before asking. You like a challenge, will meet your deadlines, and need reports showing where you are against your goal. A little applause for your stellar performance wouldn't go amiss.

Personal Considerations for ENTJs   You tend to be driven; be careful not to let your board work become a second job that takes you away from your family. Consider a nonprofit you can share with your loved ones, perhaps a zoo if you have small children, or a theater if you and your partner enjoy attending plays.

Fun Facts

- ENTJ is the second rarest type (1.8 percent), third rarest for men (2.7 percent), and rarest of all among women (0.9 percent).[38]
- Fundraisers: In a recent Association of Fundraising Professionals (AFP) survey,[39] almost a tenth (9.7 percent) of respondents were ENTJS, more than five times the 1.8 percent of ENTJs in the general population.

THE ENTREPRENEUR

Extraversion, Sensing, Thinking, Perceiving (ESTP)

ESTP Capsule Personality Description

"Flexible and tolerant, they take a pragmatic approach focused on immediate results. Theories and conceptual explanations bore them. They want to act energetically to solve the problem. Focus on the here-and-now, spontaneous, enjoy each moment that they can be active with others. Enjoy material comforts and style. Learn best through doing."[40]

The Five Steps for ESTPs

1. Thanking: Thank people when you see them socially. You'll do it spontaneously, charmingly, and, in that moment, they'll feel like the center of the universe. Let your nonprofit handle the thank-you notes to ensure they go out.
2. Engaging: You are energetic, possibly even an "adrenaline junkie." You may love sports, especially the thrill-seeking kind. If you're on the board of a sports-related or outdoors nonprofit, you may enjoy showing donors how it's done. You prize strength and competence, so ensure there's someone who'll care for less robust participants.
3. Researching: You are uncannily observant of small changes in people, facial expression, new hairdos, or broken habits. You're unapologetically pragmatic, focusing on those who can give the most the soonest. This can seem coldly calculating but may be just what your cash-strapped nonprofit needs. Focus on big shots, leaving detailed research to others. You love sharing news, so be careful not to gossip. Remember that's what's said in prospecting sessions stays in prospecting sessions.
4. Cultivating: You're in your element when working a room, where your outgoing nature and irreverent sense of humor are assets. You can make a strong, positive impression in seconds. You prefer quick, clever interchanges more than deep, philosophical tête-à-têtes anyway. You like being the center of attention and will happily take the stage to greet the crowd, present awards, or serve as master of ceremonies. Cultivation is probably your most preferred step in the fundraising process.
5. Asking: You should ask for exciting, urgently needed, and tangible projects. You relish risk and can take on donors who scare or intimidate others. This is especially true if they're someone you want to meet for your own purposes. Asking may be one of your preferred steps in the fundraising process.

ESTP's "Yeah, Buts . . ."   You'll have remarkably few hesitations, but your "yeah, buts" may include the following: "This is boring. I don't think this person's worth it. Why should I ask? What's in it for me? I don't care about feasibility studies or five-year plans. Why can't we ask for what we need here and now?"

ESTP's Asking Strengths   You can sell anything to anyone. Self-confident, assertive, and popular, you're a great storyteller, and can improvise on the spot. You have a remarkable ability to read people, to pick up on subtle, nonverbal clues. You can home in on what motivates them and persuade them to make extraordinary gifts. You're good at getting people to decide on the spot.

ESTP's Possible Weaknesses   You can fail to listen and even invent things your nonprofit doesn't do and can't deliver. If you like to shock people to get attention, you may offend some donors. You may not be comfortable with feelings, yours or other's. Sensitive donors may not be amused if you make jokes at others' expense. Your lack of preparation and penchant for winging it may cause you to misjudge your donors, offending or even causing them to stop giving.

ESTP's Best Opportunities   You respect strength and will do best asking accomplished, pragmatic businesspeople. You are energized by emergencies. Fundraise for concrete, tangible things that are urgently needed . . . like now! If you give generously and raise funds from your own contacts, you may soon be your nonprofit's star fundraiser, assigned to the most prestigious solicitations.

ESTP's Needs   You work best with accomplished, high-performing board peers who will challenge you to do your best. Although you may prefer to go it alone, bring a detail-oriented, empathetic asking partner. They can address the donor's emotional needs, answer specific questions, and follow up after the visit. In addition to major gifts, you may excel at competitive, athletic fundraising, running, swimming, or biking your way to success.

Personal Considerations for ESTP   To avoid boredom, consider serving on a board that only meets quarterly. Find a strong, dynamic executive director who'll push right back if you push him or her. You may want to serve on a prestigious board, one that offers useful business contacts and boosts your social standing. In addition to the athletic/outdoorsy causes mentioned above, you may like to serve a nonprofit where young entrepreneurs pitch you on their projects.

Fun Facts

- ESTPs make up 4.3 percent of the population; 5.6 percent of men, and 4.3 percent of women.[41]
- Fundraisers: Despite their powers of persuasion, ESTPs are under-represented in fundraising. A recent survey by the Association of Fundraising Professionals (AFP)[42] found only 1.8 percent of respondents were ESTPs, compared to 4.3 percent of the population.

THE GUARDIAN

Extraversion, Sensing, Thinking, Judging (ESTJ)

ESTJ Capsule Personality Description

"Practical, realistic, matter of fact. Decisive, quickly move to implement decisions. Organize projects and people to get things done, focus on getting results in the most efficient way possible. Take care of routine details. Have a clear set of logical standards, systematically follow them and want others to do so also. Forceful in implementing their plans."[43]

The Five Steps for ESTJs

1. Thanking: You are a responsible thanker, noting how much the donor gave and for what purpose, as well as the impact their gift made. You may include an item of special interest to each donor. You are sincerely grateful and timely with your thanks.
2. Engaging: You like encouraging donors to get more involved, to join a committee, help with public advocacy, read to children, and so forth. You will show up for a variety of engaging events. You'll connect with donors whether they attend a corporate breakfast, a press conference, or a BBQ picnic. They will look forward to seeing you and staff will appreciate your faithful participation. Engaging may be your most preferred step in the fundraising process.
3. Researching: Curious about people and their stories, you are good at making and retaining contacts. You'll determinedly read a list of 200 names to find the one who may become a lifelong supporter. You excel at research and are deservedly proud of your connections and influence. Ask staff to create profiles from online research, which

you can expand and refine through your network of knowledgeable contacts.

4. Cultivating: You like to interact with people and will enjoy your non-profit's social events. If it's a gala, you'll pitch in to sell tickets and sponsorship beforehand, welcome newcomers, and find ways they can get further involved. You're a joiner, as are your friends, many of whom you'll persuade to support your nonprofit. Cultivation may be one of your preferred steps in the fundraising process.

5. Asking: Ask donors who give as much as you do, or more. You'll be energized when soliciting pillars of the community, people of accomplishment that you admire. Accustomed to success yourself, you'll want to make best use of your time, and should choose the donors most likely to say yes to you.

ESTJ's "Yeah, Buts . . ."   May sound something like this: "I don't want them to think I'm using our friendship to get money. What will they think of me? What if they turn me down? What's the goal? This brochure seems too wishy-washy. I need to know what they'll get for their money before I can ask. What's the deadline?"

ESTJ's Asking Strengths   You'll do your homework, ask in an appropriate, thoughtful, and logical manner, and usually get a yes. Financially astute yourself, you'll want your donors to give in ways that work for them, such as spreading payments over time or liquidating assets in tax advantageous ways. You're eminently trustworthy. Donors will appreciate your follow-through.

ESTJ's Possible Weaknesses   Take care not to talk over shy donors. You may be uncomfortable with unconventional, flaky, or offbeat personalities. You are confident in your beliefs and don't like them challenged. You may argue if you feel your nonprofit is being unfairly criticized. You may generalize, and so misjudge people, especially if they are emotionally intense. Remember, people often give from their heart, not their head.

ESTJ's Best Opportunities   You value tradition and are good at celebrating milestones. You may be the perfect person to raise funds for an anniversary, to honor an outstanding citizen, or for the opening of a new facility. You like concrete projects with measurable outcomes and will do well asking corporations, foundations, and government agencies. You value sound infrastructure and will fundraise well for database upgrades, capacity-building, or long-term planning.

ESTJ's Needs   Ask to see the fundraising plan, gift acceptance policy, and volunteer job descriptions. You want to know that everyone's got a clearly defined role and is doing their part. You like to be prepared, and should get a donor profile, case statement, pledge card, and rationale before asking. You need regular progress reports and might serve well chairing the development committee of your board.

Personal Considerations for ESTJs   Avoid nonprofits that are chaotic, badly run, or fiscally unsound. If unsure, go to GuideStar (www.guide star.org/home.aspx) to review their latest 990 tax returns. You are a loyal and principled person. Once you commit, you'll stand up for your nonprofit against all comers. Make sure it's worthy of your sterling reputation before you sign on.

Fun Facts

- ESTJs make up 8.7 percent of the population; 6.3 percent of women, and 11.2 percent of men, making it the second most commonly occurring type among men.[44]
- Fundraisers: ESTJs are underrepresented in development careers. A recent Association of Fundraising Professionals (AFP) survey[45] found about half as many ESTJs in fundraising (4.8 percent) as in the general population (8.7 percent).

THE VISIONARY

Extraversion, iNtuitive, Thinking, Perceiving (ENTP)

ENTP Capsule Personality Description

"Quick, ingenious, stimulating, alert, and outspoken. Resourceful in solving new and challenging problems. Adept at generating conceptual possibilities and then analyzing them strategically. Good at reading other people, bored by routine, will seldom do the same thing the same way. Apt to turn to one new interest after another."[46]

The Five Steps for ENTPs

1. Thanking: When thanking, call the donor to mind, then write them a short note that includes one fascinating, relevant factoid they might not know. If you must look it up, so be it. You'll be that much wiser for

the activity. Don't write more than a few notes at a time and change it up, perhaps picking a different card for each person.

2. Engaging: Make engagement interesting or you won't do it. If you've brought new donors into the fold, use engaging them as an opportunity to share your nonprofit's exciting discoveries or recent breakthroughs. If you're self-employed, or a partner in a firm, engaging donors who are also clients/customers can be an efficient use of your time.

3. Researching: Pick an innovative program that interests you and find donors for that. You'll soon be an expert on who supports such projects, and why. You're great in prospect research brainstorming sessions, zoning in on those likely to yield the biggest gifts. Research may be your favorite step in the asking process.

4. Cultivating: Cultivate while you learn. For example, you might entertain donors at a lecture series, at an exhibit opening, or at a reception for a distinguished visitor. You're social enough to enjoy galas, providing you don't have to endure too much chitchat.

5. Asking: You'll enjoy fundraising for big ideas, game-changing concepts, and exciting new developments. You should ask similarly forward-thinking, intellectually bold prospects who'll fuel your flame. Avoid conservative donors fond of the status quo. Asking may be one of your most preferred steps in the fundraising process.

ENTP's "Yeah, Buts . . ."   May include the following: "I don't know if they're interested, what are we asking them to fund? I don't know how. People are sick of fundraising. No one will give. My friends will think I'm up to something. I'm not going to pretend to like someone, just to get their money."

ENTP's Asking Strengths   You understand people and can talk your way around practically any objection. You don't get mired in detail and keep donors focused on the future you envision. Donors who intimidate others don't scare you, as you're stimulated by verbal sparring and would rather be respected than liked. You're good at asking foundations and you're the match of any corporate sponsor when it comes to negotiating terms for your nonprofit.

ENTP's Possible Weaknesses   You can be impatient with donors who can't keep up. You may fail to prepare, trusting too much to your ability to think on your feet. Preferring ideas to feelings, you may miss a donor's emotional motivations. You're asking for a gift, not winning a debate. Unnecessary argument can repel conflict-averse donors.

ENTP's Best Opportunities   When it comes to funding a complex, innovative project, you can't be beat, especially if the donor or funder is your intellectual equal. You are hard to intimidate. You can solicit that crabby old man or the critical entrepreneur everyone else is afraid of. They won't hurt your feelings and you'll find the challenge invigorating.

ENTP's Needs   You bore easily, like to play with the smart kids, and abhor routine. ENTPs are the most likely type to be self-employed because they crave independence. Though coordination is necessary, ask your nonprofit to give you as much freedom and flexibility as is reasonable.

Personal Considerations for ENTPs   If you're not spending enough quality time with your family, try serving a nonprofit you can share with them. You may enjoy championing an underdog organization, one whose mission is shaking things up and challenging outmoded thinking. You may prefer a board that meets quarterly, or serving as an advisory board member, called as needed for your special skills but not responsible for ongoing management.

Fun Facts

- ENTPs make up 3.2 percent of the population, 4.0 percent of men, and 2.4 percent of women.[47]
- Fundraisers: There is a slightly higher percentage of ENTPs (4.8 percent) in fundraising than the 3.2 percent found in the general population, according to a recent Association of Fundraising Professionals (AFP) survey.[48]

FUND YOUR VISION

PUT YOUR "YES" SELF FORWARD

"Our doubts are traitors and make us lose the good we oft might win, by fearing to attempt."

—Shakespeare

Perfect heroes are no fun. We identify with those who endure trials and tribulations and must overcome daunting challenges before triumphing in the end. In chapter 1, you discovered your inner objections, the "Yeah, buts. . ." that keep you from asking. Look at that list now. Go to your profile in chapter 3 and review the "Yeah, buts" that tend to arise for your asking personality.

In addition to the recommendations for your asking profile, you can use the five-step method to turn your fears into solicitation strengths. Allow me to demonstrate with three common fears: (1) the donor won't like you, (2) you'll fail, and (3) you don't know who to ask.

I'm afraid they won't like me if I ask them for a gift. The flip side of your fear of rejection is a desire to be liked. The stronger the fear, the more likely you are to be a people pleaser. By thanking the donor thoughtfully and engaging them well, you'll show them that you care more about them than about their money. Engage your "pleaser power" to research prospects thoroughly, selecting those most likely to rally to your cause, and cultivate them until they've expressed a clear wish to do more.

After all, decades of research have shown that giving makes people happy. A 2015 article in *U.S. News and World Report*[1] notes acts of generosity increase the donor's happiness, improve the giver's physical health, and increase their longevity. The happiness we experience after helping another is called "giver's glow," according to Stephen G. Post, director of the Center for Medical Humanities, Compassionate Care, and Bioethics at New York's Stony Brook University.

Dr. Post reports that philanthropy causes the brain to release mood-elevating chemicals like dopamine and endorphins, as well as oxytocin. Oxytocin is sometimes referred to as "the love hormone" because of its association with increased social bonding, trust, and serenity. The article goes on to cite studies that found altruism reduced the mortality risk tied to stress, sometimes by as much as 63 percent. But only heartfelt, meaningful gifts yield these benefits. Contributions made grudgingly or under pressure don't have the same effect. Asking those who have been well thanked and engaged, well researched and cultivated, who give willingly, makes the donor healthier and happier.

I'm afraid they'll say no. Start by asking those who already donate, year after year. If they're going to give anyway, there's little chance you'll get turned down. Those who fear failure most are often accustomed to success, even driven by it. Harness that drive. In this chapter, you'll learn how to arrive ready for yes, not braced for a no. You'll also discover what's behind yes, no, and maybe. Sometimes the dreaded "no" exists only in your mind. Preparing mentally, emotionally, and logistically will reduce the chance you'll get turned down.

I don't know who to ask. If this is your fear, you're probably good at approaching things strategically. Use that strength. Research the donors you know until you have a sense of what would motivate them to give to your cause. Then prioritize, asking the likeliest, best prospects first. If the list is long, you may never get to the less committed ones. If you don't know a soul, build relationships with donors no one else knows, either. Think of Zofia. She was the timid plant lady in chapter 2 who thanked her way to a larger gift.

Connect with contributors whom no one knows and you'll also improve donor retention, which, as noted in chapter 2, is a critical issue for nonprofits. The Fundraising Effectiveness Report, conducted by the Association of Fundraising Professionals and the Urban Institute, states, "Taking positive steps to reduce gift and donor losses is the least expensive strategy for increasing net fundraising gains."[2] In other words, it is simpler and cheaper to keep the donors you have than to acquire new ones. Thanking those donors, getting to know them, and involving them in your nonprofit is not just a nice thing to do, it's essential to your organization's survival. By befriending unknown donors, you'll reduce attrition, raise more money, and, next year, you'll know just who to ask!

Your Asking Personality

> "I've always wanted to be somebody. Now I realize I should have been more specific."
>
> —Lily Tomlin

Your asking personality profile is based on your Myers–Briggs type. But what if your profile doesn't seem like a fit? This could occur for several reasons.

1. You might have the wrong MBTI type. Try a different test or pay for the official one offered by the Myers–Briggs Foundation. If you get the same result from different tests and still disagree, it's sometimes useful to check with your partner. Those close to you may agree with the type diagnosis, laughingly pointing out, "That's you to a tee!" If you still disagree, read the capsule descriptions of other types. If a different profile suits you better, follow the suggestions for that one.

2. Preference, not destiny. The MBTI reflects your *preferred* way of functioning in the world, but the complex and varied range of human nature, culture, family of origin, and experience cannot be reduced to four letters of the alphabet. We develop skills as we go through life and express our personality in unique ways. Take what you find useful in your asking personality profile and ignore the rest. After all, you're the expert on you.

3. You're an ambivert. The Jungian terms *extravert* and *introvert* provide handy shorthand terms to describe clusters of behaviors. Daniel Pink, author of *To Sell Is Human: The Surprising Truth about Moving Others*, uses the term *ambivert* to describe someone at the center of the introversion/extraversion continuum. Ambiverts adapt to the situations and people they encounter. Recent research by Adam Grant of the University of Pennsylvania's Wharton School of Management has found that ambiverts make the best salespeople. They know when to assert themselves and when to refrain from comment, when to speak

and when to shut up. Whether you're an introvert, an extravert, or an ambivert, my point remains the same. Ask in ways that play to your personal strengths.

Some overarching asking patterns are embedded in the quick tips chart and in-depth profiles in chapter 3. I've extracted a few, listing them below to illustrate how you can use them to work more effectively with your team.

Bringing Donors to You versus Going to Them   Introverted solicitors are often more comfortable asking on their home turf and/or at their nonprofit rather than at a restaurant or at their donor's place of work. This allows analytic introverts to demonstrate the concrete need for funding and more emotional introverts to share their experience with donors. Extraverts like to ask on-site but are also able to ask in the location that's most convenient for their donor.

Facts versus Feelings   More analytic types like to absorb, digest, and discuss data. They may prep by reviewing the plan, measurable outcomes, goals, timelines, and budgets. It makes them feel safe and gives them confidence. The same level of detail can overwhelm more emotional types. The latter may prep better with a few, key bullet points, and/or by steeping themselves in the experience of their nonprofit.

Theoretical Future versus Tangible Present   I have found iNtuitive thinkers, such as ENTJs (the Executive), INTJs (the Strategist), INTPs (the Philosopher), and ENTPs (the Visionary), enjoy pitching strategic plans and innovative theories. More pragmatic types may lose patience with conceptual projects that are years from implementation. The practical ESTPs (the Entrepreneur), ESTJs (the Guardian), ISTJs (the Good Steward), and ISTPs (the Craftsman) prefer fundraising for concrete projects, needed right here and now.

Talking versus Listening   Many extraverts are articulate, persuasive, and can make a compelling case. In their enthusiasm, they sometimes interrupt or talk over donors. They need to practice listening. Introverts may have a harder time connecting initially but are often excellent and attentive listeners. They pick up on subtle clues, learn about donors, and provide them with the time and space they need to decide.

The last section of each asking personality profile, Personal Considerations, explains how to choose the right board for you.

Some volunteers idealize nonprofits, assuming they're populated by noble souls. They anticipate a cooperative and inspiring board experience. Most of the time, that's what they find. Yet nonprofits, like churches, businesses, and government agencies, are made up of people, good and bad, generous and selfish, competent and inept. Nonprofit staff function in challenging environments, often overworked, underpaid, and keenly aware of unmet needs.

Seek a culture fit, as well as a mission fit, when choosing a board. If you're conflict adverse, steer clear of organizations where the board chair is feuding with the executive director. If you hate playing politics, avoid nonprofits rife with it. If you're timid, don't join a board led by an authoritarian bully. Since it can be hard to know these things in advance, sit in on a board meeting before joining or try volunteering. Scope things out, observe, and question the staff and volunteers. Joining the right team is critical to becoming the best fundraiser you can be.

The "You" Who Shows Up

"We choose our joys and sorrows long before we experience them."

—Kahlil Gibran

Let's say you've completed the steps, are playing to your strengths, know who you're asking, what they care about, and how much to request. You're ready to ask but not feeling great. In fact, you're miserable. You're exhausted, behind on a report for work, and can't find your glasses.

Stop.

If you're frazzled or depressed, your donor will sense it. Your mood sets the tone for the asking conversation. If you're happy, you'll get more gifts. So get happy!

What?

That's right. I said get happy.

There's a science to happiness and you can learn it. Shawn Achor, one of the most popular lecturers at Harvard and author of *The Happiness Advantage,* has challenged our traditional approach to happiness. Most of us think that if we succeed, get the right job, lose the extra pounds, find our true love, *then* we'll be happy. Achor's research demonstrates the opposite. If we get happy first, we become more successful in almost every area of our lives. When we're positive, our brains become more engaged, creative, motivated, energetic, resilient, and productive. Achor has distilled the art of happiness down to a few simple principles.

For one, it seems our grandparents were right. If you count your blessings you will be a happier person. Create your own happiness journal. Every day, note something for which you're grateful. To avoid repetition (my husband, my kids, etc.), describe something that's occurred in the last twenty-four hours: the neighbor who shoveled your driveway unasked, the waitress who made you laugh, the man who helped you catch your train.

Our lives are full of meaning, but we rarely stop to notice or appreciate it. Take a moment. Think of something meaningful you experienced in the last twenty-four hours and write it down. It might be a crocus poking up through the snow, the contented murmur of a sleeping child, a winsome cloud formation, or evocative line in a book. Simply attending to and acknowledging meaning will make you happier and more satisfied.

Next, Achor recommends you perform a random act of kindness, every day, for someone who won't be able to return the favor. No matter how limited our means, we all have the power to help others. For example, on Sunday afternoons, my mother used to visit a lonely widow in an old age home. My parents had little money to raise the seven of us, yet every week my mom brought her elderly friend some little gift, a plant, barrettes for her hair, or a funny picture. At the time, I saw this as proof of my mom's sainthood. Though my mother was a wonderful person, I now understand those visits cheered her as much as they did her elderly friend.

Here's another happiness tip. Before you ask, take a walk in the fresh air, jump on your bike, or even skip rope in your office. As little as fifteen minutes of physical exercise will elevate your mood.

Try meditation. People who meditate are happier than those who don't. If you're not trained in meditation, sit in a quiet place and watch your breath go in and out for two minutes. It's calming, will center you, and put you in a better frame of mind to ask. Studying meditation has improved my fundraising performance more than anything else I've ever done.

As noted above, giving makes you happy. Make your own gift, donating as generously as you can to get an optimal "giver's glow," before asking others.

Scan yourself before you ask. Check that you've thanked and engaged your donor or researched and cultivated your prospect. Make your own stretch gift. Imagine your donor smiling and welcoming, excited to hear about your cause, eager to help. If you arrive calm, happy, and expecting a yes, your donor will respond and be more likely to grant your request.

ACTIVITY: Get Happy

Fill out this Happiness Journal sheet (table 4.1). Make as many copies as you like. Doing this daily will increase your overall happiness quotient, whether you're fundraising or not.

Table 4.1. Happiness Journal ©VMJA 2018

Activity	Happiness Journal date: _____
I'm grateful for this:	
I found this meaningful:	
My random act of kindness was:	
My fifteen-minute exercise was:	
I meditated today. (List any reflections/ insights.)	

GET THE APPOINTMENT AND GET READY

"Success comes when people act together; failure tends to happen alone"

—Deepack Chopra

The basic steps of asking are simple. You get the appointment, prepare for the visit, discuss your nonprofit, ask for the gift, receive the donor's decision, agree on next steps, say thank you, leave, and follow up. The first step, getting the appointment, can be the most intimidating, so let's unpack that.

Make It Easy with Pre-ask Visits   Scheduling an asking visit is much easier if it's not your first call. In the five steps, I've emphasized the need for pre-ask visits, thanking, engaging donors, and cultivation visits with prospects. If you've already met, getting an asking date is just another call. It's an important one, though. According to master fundraiser Jerald Panas, research shows that once you've secured the asking appointment, you're 85 percent of the way to getting a gift.

Write First   Write a brief letter or email requesting the visit and letting your donor know you'll call to follow up. Include a deadline in your note, such as, "I'll call you by Thursday, February 8, to find a time that works." You can describe the purpose of the visit in your letter or email, which may prompt the donor to respond before you even call. I send several letters at once. It's more efficient and allows me to cluster my follow-up calls.

Block Out Potential   Book asking visit times in your calendar and have those dates handy before you call. Review background info on your donors, including a photo of them, if possible. Jot down a few talking points for each call. My colleague, Mark Pittman, has a refreshingly simple approach. His index-card script contains just three points:

1. Ask if it's an OK time to talk.
2. Get the appointment.
3. Get off the phone!

The purpose of the call is to calendar some time together, not to ask for the gift.

Emotional Prep   I've mentioned the importance of getting happy before asking, and that includes asking to visit. Stand, or even walk around when making your call, and smile. They won't see you, but they'll hear the warmth in your voice. Some of us develop little rituals before calling. For example, I pass a picture of my kids over my phone, which somehow gives me confidence and makes me laugh. I bring that lightness to the call.

The Call   Set aside a block of time to make calls. Start with the easiest ones: those likely to say yes. You'll be less anxious and get comfortable with what you're saying. Making several calls, one after the other, also increases the odds you'll reach a live person. If you only make one call and strike out, it's easy to get discouraged. When a donor picks up, tell them you're following up on the email (or letter) you sent, as promised. Be prepared to leave messages. Donors are more likely to return your call if your message indicates you'll phone again at a specific time. Speaking of specifics, don't ask if they'll meet, but rather when. "Would you prefer to meet Monday at noon or Thursday after work?"

Confirmation When someone agrees to a visit, confirm the date via email and by sending a digital meeting invite through iTunes or Google Calendar. When the donor accepts the digital appointment, it goes right into their calendar. The software will tell them if they've accidentally double-booked themselves. If so, it will prompt them to choose another time. A digital appointment also allows you to include time, place, and contact info, such as your cell phone number, to avoid uncertainty later.

Possible Objections to Meeting If you've worked the steps, most people you call will be glad to hear from you and willing to meet. Sometimes, though, you'll encounter objections ranging from, "I'll gladly give, you don't have to visit," to "You can come if you like, but I'm not giving you a dime." You saw how we handled the second scenario with the crabby advocate in chapter 2. But how about other objections? Here are some examples and how to handle them.

Donor: I'll give but we don't need to meet. I don't want to take up your valuable time.

You: Thank you. I appreciate your consideration, and I'd still like to come. Visiting with supporters like you is one of the best parts of my job as a board member. It would help me lead more wisely, make better decisions, if I could hear your take on how we're doing. How about coffee before work next Thursday or . . .

Donor: I'm too busy to meet in person; let's meet by phone.

You: If you let me stop by, I promise I won't take more than twenty minutes. After that, you can kick me out! It would help me to hear your feedback, and I can get a better sense of your thoughts if we chat in person. I could swing by Wednesday at 1 p.m. or . . .

Donor: Why don't you send me the materials and I'll let you know what I think?

You: Great! I'll mail it today, so you'll have time to review it over the weekend. Can you tell me what you think of it over lunch Wednesday? We're discussing this initiative at our next board meeting, and I'd like your input by then, if possible.

Donor: Can I think about it and get back to you?

You: Of course. Maybe it would help if I came over with Dr. Wagner, our executive director. I'd love you to meet him, and he'll be able to answer any questions you have. Then you can think it over and let us know what you decide. He could see us if we swing by the museum Wednesday at 5 or . . .

Where to Meet Conventional wisdom tells us to meet donors in the place that's most convenient for them. I do this when necessary, but I prefer to meet donors at my nonprofit. It's harder to get such meetings. You may be asking a donor to go beyond their comfort zone, but "nothing sells the zoo like the zoo!" Although restaurants provide a neutral common ground, a donor can be hailed by colleagues or interrupted by waiters, disrupting the flow of the conversation. At a minimum, I have a 3-2-1 rule. First, I try three times to get a meeting at my nonprofit. If that fails, I try twice to schedule our meeting at a neutral location, such as a quiet restaurant. Only after these have failed do I offer to meet at their home or workplace.

I once called twenty corporate executives I'd met just to find one who'd watch a play with me and a hundred kindergarteners in an elementary school cafeteria at eight in the morning. Our theater's outreach had created a Native American–themed show, with lots of playful interaction designed to meet learning objectives for five-year-old children.

This businessman later told me it was the best part of his week . . . possibly his month!

Thanks to that visit, his company "adopted" the entire school district. They paid for every student to see a performance. Our actors performed at the elementary school for the little kids, while the older students came to our theater to attend full-length plays. My guest continued to champion the program he'd started, ensuring the company's support for years afterward.

Hopefully your prospects and donors know your nonprofit well by the time you get to the fifth step. But if they haven't yet experienced it, make that part of the asking process.

As I said, most experts recommend you ask at the location that's most convenient to the donor. But what about accommodating the askers? Use your powers of persuasion to get your donor to your nonprofit. Those who come will have a richer experience, be more likely to give, and to give generously, if you immerse them in the transformative power of your cause.

Prepare for the Visit

"It usually takes more than three weeks to prepare a good impromptu speech."

—Mark Twain

Getting ready to ask is much like preparing to call for the appointment. Use your five-step checklist to ensure you've thanked and engaged past donors and researched and cultivated prospects. Review the donor/prospect's profile and the materials about your nonprofit. Make sure you know how much you're requesting, have a pledge card, an FAQ sheet, the address, and the donor's phone number. Check that you're in a good mood and voilà! You're off.

Let's run through that again.

Five-Step Checklist

Donors   If you're asking a donor, check that they've been thanked properly for their last gift. If you're the one who asked, you may want to reread a copy of the thank-you note you sent. Next, check that your donor's been well engaged and has gotten more involved since their last gift. Did someone tell them what your nonprofit did with their money? If you don't know, check with staff. If *they're* not sure, do so yourself. Tell the donor the impact they made. It can be as simple as a brief email, and staff can tell you what to say.

Prospects   If they've not given before, check that they've been researched and cultivated to the point of giving.

Donor/Prospect Info   Refresh your memory before your call. If you already know the person you're asking, this is easy. Just skim their recent giving history and bio. If you don't know them, or they're new to your nonprofit, you may want a bit more information, their giving to others, connection to your nonprofit, and any notes on what might motivate them to give.

Your nonprofit's development director is like a traffic cop. They indicate who goes where in what order, ensuring the right person asks the right person for the right thing at the right time. Ask fundraising staff to guide you and keep them in the loop. In addition to providing background info, they can help develop the right strategy for approaching each donor.

Donor/Prospect Ask Amount   Know how much you'll be requesting before your visit. This should have been determined with board peers and confirmed by staff, perhaps in a prospect rating session.

Info about Your Nonprofit   Depending on your asking personality, you may want to review lots of material, brochures, plans, drawings, and budgets. Or, you may prefer to hit the highlights, skimming, but not getting bogged down in detail. Whatever your approach, make sure you can describe your nonprofit and what you're asking for, and be sure to bring a pledge card. You may also wish to bring a one-page sheet with answers to frequently asked questions, often called an FAQ. The FAQ describes your main programs, numbers of constituents served, lists the board of directors, your operating budget, and other basic info. You may think you know this, but if you're nervous, random questions can take you off guard, stopping you like a deer caught in headlights. Better to carry an FAQ cheat sheet, just in case.

Pledge Card or Payment Form In your excitement at getting a big gift, it's easy to forget to ask how the donor wants to pay, when they'll do so, whether they want reminders, and so forth. Completing the form will prompt them to address each of these points.

Helpful Tips for Emotional/Physical Prep If you follow the five steps, play to your strengths, and get happy, you'll be in the right frame of mind to ask. Still, even experienced fundraisers feel a bit anxious at this point. If you do, here are a few tips that may help:

- Visualization has helped athletes around the world. You may use negative visualization without realizing it. It's called worrying. By imagining failure, you make it more likely, so visualize success instead. Close your eyes, calm your mind, and observe your breath for a couple of minutes. Picture your donor welcoming you warmly and listening intently. Imagine that he or she has just gotten a bonus and donates generously. Steeped in positive images, you'll approach your visit in a calmer, more confident frame of mind.
- Wear comfortable clothes. It's hard to feel buoyant with new shoes pinching your toes or a waistband that keeps riding up. If your clothes make you fidget, you'll distract your donor as well as yourself. Dress nicely, but comfortably.
- Don't eat, or do so sparingly, before your visit. This is a common practice among actors, who rarely eat before going onstage. You'll feel lighter and more alert if you're not weighed down by a heavy meal. Plus, you won't need to decline your host's offer of refreshments because you're stuffed.
- Develop a script and practice. Write down what you plan to say and practice it in front of your mirror or with a friend or fellow board member. You won't follow your script exactly, but the words will flow more smoothly if you've said them a few times.

ACTIVITY: Email and Phone Script

Draft your previsit email and phone script for scheduling your visit. You'll find examples of each in the Toolkit section of this book.

LISTEN YOUR WAY TO MAJOR GIFTS

"Drawing on my fine command of the language, I said nothing."

—Robert Benchley

Asking for a gift usually includes the following elements: the opening, discussion of your nonprofit, including making the case for support, asking for the gift, the donor's decision, next steps, closure, and follow-up. One of the most important, effective, and difficult lessons to learn in fundraising is to keep your mouth shut. The asking outline below includes several points where I suggest you listen. It also indicates where you should ask a question to move the conversation forward.

Opening

Begin by reiterating the reason for meeting and confirming how much time you have. Allow a few minutes of small talk and to catch up on family and friends you may have in common. Then share (briefly) your own motivation. For example, "You know, as I was driving over, I remembered my first camping trip with my dad. . . ."

Transition Question: "So, what sparked your interest in XYZ Nonprofit?"

Discuss Your Nonprofit

Listen to your donor/prospect's response. Pay attention to anything that relates to your proposal. Summarize your nonprofit's situation, making two to three simple points. Allow space for your donor/prospect to comment on each. For example,

- "XYZ Nonprofit helps single moms achieve financial independence. How important do you think that is, given the current economic climate?" Listen to their response.
- "These moms can't work without reliable daycare, so XYZ helps them secure subsidized care near their jobs/homes. What do you think of that strategy?" Listen.
- "You've built your own business up from scratch. XYZ is helping these moms create and run small businesses. This makes it easier for them to juggle earning a living with taking care of their families. What advice would you give them?" Listen.

Transition Question: "Do you have any questions or concerns about XYZ Nonprofit that you'd like to discuss?"

Ask for the Gift

If they've given in the past, thank them again for their support; remind them of how much they gave before, and the impact their gift made. Invite them to consider giving again.

How much should you request? If it's an annual gift, the rule of thumb is to suggest a figure that's a bit more than the amount they gave last year. Studies show that you secure larger gifts when you ask for a specific amount, or at least a range, than when you leave it open ended. It's generally unwise to ask them to give "whatever you feel is right." This leaves them floundering if they're unsure what's expected of them. Lacking this knowledge, they may name a low figure, just to be on the safe side.

A pyramid of gifts can be helpful here. Indicate a couple of levels and suggest, "It would be great if you could give in this range." That way, they know what's expected of them. They can give on the high end if they're feeling generous, or on the low side without losing face.

The request is the transition question. Here's an example.

Transition Question: "Joan and I have pledged half the cost of a new playground, so the kids can run around in the fresh air while their moms are in class. Would you consider joining us by making a gift of $10,000?"

Stop. Let your donor think.

This is the hard part.

Western culture abhors a silence. Use this to your advantage. Your donor may feel compelled to fill the gap by explaining or thinking it through aloud, sharing their reasons why they will or won't give, how they feel about the amount you've named, the project, or the timing.

If they don't answer, you may get anxious, even backpedal: "But I'll understand if it's too much, or a bad time, or if you're not interested. . . ."

Don't do it.

Let them answer.

They are grown-ups and can make their own choices. You don't have the right to preempt their decision. It belongs to them.

Their Decision

If they say "yes," congratulations! If appropriate, have them write a check and/or fill out the pledge form, thank them, and confirm any next steps. You may wish to invite them to your next event before saying farewell.

If they say "maybe," don't say anything. Look at them attentively and give them a chance to elaborate. Your job is to learn what stands between them and their decision. Sometimes "maybe" means, "I have to talk to my partner (or financial advisor)." Sometimes maybe means, "I need time to think about it." If they don't elaborate, explore a little. Ask, "Do you need more time? Is there somebody you want to consult? Do you have additional questions you need answered? Should I touch base in a month to see if this becomes clearer to you?" Try to discover what they need and help them, if you can. Before you leave, agree on next steps.

If they say "no," don't speak. You'll want to hear what comes next.

One of my board solicitors, Ben, was turned down by a donor. Ben remained quiet, looking at the donor in a supportive way, clearly wanting to hear more. In the silence, the donor spoke his thoughts. "You see Ben, I'm paying for my daughter's wedding, so there's no way I can make a gift now. Though I'd like to. I mean, I really like what you're doing. I guess you need the money now. But if you didn't . . . in three months, she'll be married, and I could donate something by the end of the year. I liquidated stock to pay for the wedding, so I might need a tax deduction in December. How much did you say you wanted?"

Ben repeated the amount, suggesting his friend could pledge now, and pay it over three years. The donor signed the pledge form, making the gift in honor of the newlyweds!

If you start by asking current, well-thanked, and engaged donors, you'll rarely hear no. Follow the five steps and play to your strengths. Usually, you'll be asking those ready to say yes. But things change, and people can surprise you. You may get a no, which can be awkward.

If the person you're visiting can't give, for financial or personal reasons, accept their decision graciously, but continue to seek their support. Ask them, "If you could help, would you want to?" Often, they'll respond in the affirmative. If they do, suggest they volunteer, lend a hand in the office, or promote your cause as a social media ambassador. Don't leave them feeling embarrassed or that you only want them for their money. Engage them as valued members of the team. Even if they're too busy to volunteer, or are not interested, it's flattering to be asked.

They may say no without telling you why and decline your efforts to learn more or to involve them. If so, tell them your organization's always trying to improve. Ask if there's anything you can do to earn their support. Whatever their response, listen carefully, and repeat their concerns back to them to confirm you've understood. This will also help you remember what they said. Don't argue with them, even if you think they're wrong. Respond thoughtfully. Thank them for their honesty and their time. If there's been a misunderstanding, you can regroup with staff and decide how to address it later.

Transition Question: Whatever their decision, repeat it back to them and ask, "Have I understood you correctly?"

Next Steps, Closure, and Follow-Up

Once you've confirmed their decision, agree on next steps.

Yes: If they've made a gift, have them fill out the form, say thank you, tell them they'll get an acknowledgment for tax purposes, and invite them to your nonprofit's next program or event. Reiterate anything you've promised to do for them, such as send information or tickets.

Maybe: If they say maybe, summarize what you understand their position to be, note any follow-up on your part, and suggest engagement opportunities they might enjoy while considering your request.

No: If they've declined to give, thank them for their time and honesty. Repeat what you understand to be the situation. If you've agreed on any follow-up steps, such as getting answers to specific questions, mention those as well.

Transition Question: "Is there anything more I can do for you or questions I can answer before I go?"

Listen. If they bring up anything new, sit down again and address these new issues if you can. By this point, you'll usually have covered everything and be on your way.

Whatever their decision, send a thank-you note or email summarizing the meeting. It's polite and provides your donor with an opportunity to comment on, correct, or expand on what happened before their decision is cast in stone. Copy or resend it to your development director so that they'll know what happened and have a record for the file.

ACTIVITY: Asking Script

Create your own asking script using the example above. You'll find a template in the Fundraiser's Toolkit section of this book.

ASK AS A TEAM

> "Set your life on fire. Seek those who fan your flames."
>
> —Rumi

When it comes to asking, two heads are better than one.

Asking with a partner can make you twice as successful, especially if they have a personality that complements your own. An introvert may notice important details an extravert misses, while an extravert may convey a more exciting and compelling vision of the future.

Asking with a member of staff has many advantages. You'll have an expert on hand to answer in-depth questions, and most nonprofit CEOs and development officers are experienced solicitors. Donors may be eager to meet your executive director, learning about your nonprofit right from the horse's mouth, so to speak. Asking with a development officer ensures you'll have someone who can help you prep beforehand and to handle postvisit follow-up tasks. Program staff can also be great asking partners, sharing vivid tales of their work on the front lines, whether it's cheetah conservation or helping unemployed dads get their GEDs.

Asking with a partner follows the same steps as solo asking, with a few variations.

1. *Find your asking personalities and discuss.* If you know your asking personalities, you can prepare in ways that play to each solicitor's strengths. A more extraverted partner may get the appointment, while the more analytical partner reviews the background material.
2. *Ask donors before prospects.* It takes a little extra practice to get the rhythm of asking with a partner. Develop fluency by doing the easiest solicitations first, regular donors who'll give even if you stumble a bit. This will build your confidence as an asking team.
3. *Get the appointment.* Obviously, you'll need to block out times you're both free before scheduling the appointment. Who should request the visit? The partner most likely to get a yes! Sometimes that's the

person closest to the donor, but sometimes it's the partner the donor hasn't met, such as the executive director or a theater's star actor. Digital scheduling is particularly helpful when coordinating several individuals. Your development director may be willing to help coordinate multiple parties. Most important, don't surprise your donor with an unexpected visitor. If you're coming with the executive director, say so, and why. For example, "When I told John I was seeing you about outreach, he asked if he could come along. He'd like to share some exciting progress we've made. Would it be okay if he joined us?" Meeting with your donors at your nonprofit makes it easier for staff to join part, or all, of the conversation.

4. *Prepare for the visit together.* Make sure donors have been thanked and engaged and prospects researched and cultivated. Take a moment to review their bio, giving history, and involvement, and to share your knowledge with your partner. For example, one of you may know Susan majored in anthropology, the other that she's interested in serving immigrants. Agree on how much you'll request and for what purpose. Brief yourselves in the way that suits each of you best. Don't forget to prepare emotionally and physically as well, get happy, wear comfortable clothes, and envision success.

5. *Develop a script and practice.* You don't want to stop in the middle of a visit to stare at your partner, wondering which of you is supposed to ask for the gift. Rough out the conversational steps—opening, discussion of your nonprofit, your request, their decision, next steps, closure, and follow-up—along with transition questions. Role-play your donor's possible answers. When you're practicing, you might even throw out a silly response or two, just to loosen up before your visit.

6. *Asking visit.* Confirm your appointment the day before and give yourself extra time to get there. Decide which of you will watch the clock, ensuring you don't run out of time before asking. Agree who will ask, who will tackle any difficult questions, and how you'll deal with a yes, no, or maybe. Decide who'll reiterate any agreed-upon next steps and take the pledge form, if it's been completed. After the visit, give yourself time to compare notes with your partner. It's amazing how often two people in the same meeting hear different things and may even remember the result differently. Agree in advance which of you will recap the visit in a thank-you email and remember to copy your partner and your nonprofit when you do.

"Help! I Chair the Development Committee!"

"The important work of moving the world forward does not wait to be done by perfect men."

—George Elliot

At most nonprofits, the development committee of the board, supported by staff, is responsible for fundraising. But it's hard to do a good job if you don't know what your job is! To complicate matters, the role of the development committee varies by nonprofit. Large, prestigious organizations employ hundreds of fundraising professionals, some dedicated to supporting board members, through every stage of the asking process. At small nonprofits, one part-time development officer may do all the fundraising, leaving them little time to assist the board.

Whatever the size of your nonprofit, you'll chair your committee more effectively if you know what a development office does and how to work with it.

What a Development Department Does (and Does Not) Do   It may surprise you to learn that many successful fundraising professionals rarely ask individuals to give. More often, they work behind the scenes. They ensure that the right person asks the right person at the right time to fund the right project for the right amount, so that the donor gives and everyone's happy. Your nonprofit's development department creates and implements the fundraising plan for the year. They conduct research, prepare communication materials, send appeals, coordinate volunteers, plan and execute events, and write and submit grant proposals. Your fundraising staff may solicit corporations, foundations, and government agencies directly, but they may still need you to leverage your connections and provide entrée.

Many boards (and even nonprofit CEOs) think they can hire a hotshot professional fundraiser to ask for gifts so they don't have to. This doesn't work. Why not?

There are several good reasons.

First, it's hard to build long-term relationships between your nonprofit and donors if their only contact is with development staff. In 2013, *Underdeveloped: A National Study of Challenges Facing Nonprofit Fundraising*[3] found most development offices contained revolving doors. Development directors are expected to leave their jobs in less than two years and 40 percent are expected to leave the field of fundraising entirely. The study found that once vacated, development director positions remained unfilled for six months or more.

Imagine the friend who donates to your charity being visited by a different fundraiser every other year. "Why doesn't Joe come see me himself?" they may wonder. "I guess this isn't very important to him." Your involvement is critical to building long-term donor relationships.

Second, you'll budget contributed revenue more cautiously if you have skin in the game, if you're at least partly responsible for bringing in gifts. Budgeting revenue from donors should be based on realistic projections based on their track records, capacity, and interest; on qualified prospects in the pipeline, not wishful thinking. The more involved you are in the fundraising process, the more realistic your budgeting will be.

Third, donors know development professionals are paid to ask, whereas you are not. They know you're donating your time, expertise, and money. You offer your personal guarantee that your charity is worthy, you testify to its impact, and you promise their gifts will be used wisely.

What the Development Committee Does   The purpose of the development committee is to raise the funds needed to fulfill your nonprofit's mission. You'll meet regularly, perhaps monthly. With staff, you'll present the year's fundraising plan to the board as part of the budget for the coming fiscal year. Your committee may be composed of individuals, each of whom may lead a different fundraising initiative. For example, you might lead the board giving campaign, another member of the committee may chair corporate giving, a third may chair the gala, a fourth the annual fund, and a fifth the major gift society.

Alternately, or additionally, you can structure your committee according to everyone's preferred steps, with thanking, engaging, researching, cultivation, and asking chairs.

Moves Management   The committee leads the board and staff in taking prospects and donors through the five steps. This is sometimes called moves management, because there's always a next move in the solicitation process, even if the move is deciding a prospect's not right for your cause and should go in the "do not pursue" file. The first moves are to thank and engage donors who've already given.

Prospect Research   For those who've not yet given, research is the first move. You'll review names of prospective donors to identify those who may be interested in supporting your cause. You'll estimate how much they might give, who knows them, and how they might be approached. When leading a prospect research session, ask the group, "What's our next step here?" If you don't know a prospect, ask who might make an introduction. If they haven't responded to invitations, ask whether you should continue to pursue them or focus elsewhere. Moves management also includes cultivation, introducing prospective donors to your nonprofit to see if they are interested in getting more involved. The final step in moves management is asking, which is easy when you're approaching well-engaged donors and thoroughly cultivated prospects.

Someone, usually a member of staff, will take minutes during research and rating sessions, noting who is assigned to which prospects/donors and who will do what by when. Each committee member should leave with a list of individuals to which they're assigned, and action steps to move each constituent a bit closer to your cause.

Inspire through Experience   At the start of each development committee meeting, find vivid ways to immerse your team in your nonprofit's purpose. Be creative. Brainstorm possibilities with staff. For example, if you serve a school for the blind, you might have your committee navigating through a classroom blindfolded. If you serve a museum, pass around an unusual artifact and learn the story of its acquisition and significance from your curator. Invite a new homeowner to tell the story of how your nonprofit helped make their dream come true. Better yet, hold your meeting in a soon-to-be-completed house. Make every meeting different and, if possible, tie these activities to your fundraising goals. Your sessions will become memorable, and you'll raise more money.

Goal Setting

"Ah, but a man's reach must exceed his grasp or what's a heaven for?"

—Robert Browning

With staff, you'll develop fundraising goals. To do so, you'll ask the following questions:

How much do we *need* to raise? Often the same as the current year, plus a bit more.

How much do we *want* to raise? This includes funding for growth and new initiatives.

How much *can* we raise? This is where you challenge yourself, possibly investing in new software, outsourcing grantswriting, or adding staff to increase your fundraising capacity. You may choose to communicate two goals: a safe goal for the budget, and a second, more ambitious stretch goal. The important thing is to set goals and revisit progress at each meeting.

There are proven ways to use goals to improve your team's performance.

1. *Allow responsible parties to provide input when establishing their goals.* For example, let the gala chair propose how much they think they can deliver next year. Have the corporate chair consult with staff, calculating how much they might secure from current and prospective sponsors or how increasing benefit levels might affect revenue before asking them to budget sponsorship revenue for the upcoming year.

2. *Write goals and decide on actions, commit, and report back.* Ask each committee member to write down their personal fundraising goal, as well as the action steps they will take to achieve it. Have them tell a supportive peer that they will achieve this goal and suggest that they determine progress every two weeks. These steps—writing goals, action steps declaring your commitment to a third party, and reporting back to the team—have been demonstrated to increase performance more than 75 percent, according to a study conducted by Dominican University.[4]

3. *Harness goals to interests and passion.* All organizations need unrestricted gifts, but if someone's willing to champion a program, make that their goal. For example, a committee member with celiac disease may fundraise to offer gluten-free options at your food cupboard.

4. *Set goals that play to your strengths:* If you structure your committee by its members' preferred steps, a thanking chair, an engagement chair, a research chair, and so forth, consider setting goals for each step. The thanking chair's goals might include ensuring everyone is thanked by email within twenty-four hours, that donors receive an official thank-you letter for tax purposes within two weeks, and that all $1,000+ donors get a thank-you call or visit within three months of contributing. The engagement committee chair might have a goal of scheduling "touch base" calls to your nonprofit's top hundred donors within the next six months. The research chair's goals might include identifying seventy-five prospects, each capable of giving $1,000 or more. The cultivation chair's goal might be to bring thirty-five of these prospects to an activity within the year. The asking chair's goal might be to solicit twenty of these well-researched and cultivated prospects.

Whatever your goals, make sure they're quantifiable and can be tracked without unduly burdening your staff. To share progress and hold yourself accountable, you may wish to use software such as idonethis (https://home.idonethis.com) or stickK (www.stickk.com). Companies such as mycom mittee.com (http://mycommittee.com/Solutions/ForNonProfitOrganiza-tions/tabid/216/Default.aspx) and Board Effect (www.boardeffect.com) offer software designed to help you manage your development committee, keeping everyone on track with their tasks.

ACTIVITY: Update Your Job Description

Review and update your development committee job description. If it doesn't exist, create one. You'll find a sample and links to additional re-sources in the Fundraiser's Toolkit at the end of this book.

PLAN YOUR CAMPAIGN

"Failing to plan is planning to fail."

—Alan Lakein

The Development Plan

The development plan is your roadmap to a fully funded future. Yet according to *Underdeveloped: A National Study of Challenges Facing Non-profit Fundraising,* 23 percent of nonprofits have no fundraising plan at all in place.[5]

It's important to lay a course that's easy to understand, adjust, and implement.

Much of your fundraising will be the same each year, the annual appeal, the gala, the usual round of grant applications and reports. There will be changes you can anticipate, such as a multiyear grant ending, and there will be unexpected detours. You might receive a request for proposal (RFP) from a new funder and scramble to apply by their deadline. Or a big donor may give elsewhere, leaving a $50,000 hole in your budget.

I am a big fan of the one-page development plan. If you don't have a plan, because your nonprofit's too small or understaffed, you can create a one-pager over lunch. If you lead a larger organization that uses a long and in-depth plan, ask your development director to summarize it for commit-tee use. (See table 4.2 for an example of such a plan.) The left column lists sample campaigns, board giving, major gifts, annual fund, grants, sponsor-ship, and a gala. There's even a row for an as-yet unplanned 5K run. Each campaign has a designated leader and dollar goal. At a glance, your com-mittee can see what should happen each month. Build prospecting and vol-unteer recruitment into the schedule as well as planning and goal setting.

Table 4.2. Sample One-Page Development Plan (Completed) ©VMJA 2018

Campaigns	July	August	September	October	November
Board campaign ____Chair $____ Goal	Develop board ask ltr & set ask amounts	Send board appeal letter	Appeal at board meeting	Board chair follow-up	Year-end board campaign wrap-up
Major gifts $1,000 + donors ____Chair $____ Goal	Develop materials, ID, research, rate & set approach for $1K+ donors	Board pick prospect/ donors to cultivate & solicit	Schedule times for behind-the-scenes visits	Invite donors to holiday events. Personalize appeal letters	Appeals go out
Annual fund <$1,000 donors & prospects ____Chair $____ Goal	Develop back-to-school appeal & materials	Drop fall appeal	Board members choose donors. Add personal notes (assign if necessary)	Send holiday gift promo letter with pre-ask email	Holiday appeal drops
Grants— Corporate, foundation & government (staff leads) $____ Goal	HCA proposal— internal deadline 7/10, external deadline 7/31	PCF proposal— internal deadline 8/15; ABC Foundation report due 8/19	PCF proposal — external deadline 9/15; TCF internal deadline 9/30	TCF external deadline 10/30; DRFS Foundation internal deadline 10/17	DRFS external deadline 11/14
Corporate sponsorship ____Chair $____ Goal	Schedule visits to unsecured current & new sponsors	Finalize season-opening sponsor benefits	Season opening		Finalize holiday show sponsors
Gala _____ & ____Chair $____ Goal	Make & send gala sponsor packets		Visits to secure gala sponsors	Send "save-the-date" cards	Auction committee solicits items
Proposed 5K run ____Chair $____ Goal	TBD	TBD	TBD	TBD	TBD

December	January	February	March	April	May	June
	New board members recruited & asked	Review prospects w/new board members				Review this year, set next year's goals
Solicitor follow-up and/or thanks at holiday show	Schedule spring visits & draft spring appeal	Cultivation visits	Cultivation visits. Spring appeal goes out	Spring appeal follow-up	Send invites to next month's event	Set next year's $ and site visit goals
Follow-up year-end e-appeals	Prep snail mail appeal to lapsed donors	Send snail mail appeal to lapsed donors, w/pre- & post-appeal emails	Develop crowd funding appeal	Launch crowd-funding campaign	Wrap up crowd-funding campaign & send thanks	Assess this year; set strategy and goals for next year
DAL Report due 12/5	VCA proposal—internal deadline 1/15; MCL proposal—internal deadline 1/8	VCA proposal—external deadline 2/14; MCL proposal—external deadline 2/8	BJS proposal & report—internal deadlines	BJS proposal & report—external deadlines 4/18	Identify new prospects for next year	Set next year's goals
Holiday show	Sponsor reports out		Develop next year's sponsor benefit packages	Invite current sponsors to renew for next year	Schedule personal visits to secure current sponsors	Send intro packets to new potential sponsors
Board & committee sell tickets	Confirm & advertise auction items	Push to sell tickets & finalize logistics	Gala	Gala debrief & thanks	Recruit next year's co-chairs & committee	Develop next year's theme & goal
TBD	TBD	TBD	TBD	TBD	TBD	TBD

Each grant is assigned an internal deadline that occurs a month before the funder's deadline. Since most of us submit proposals at the last minute, applying early will impress your funders. It will also provide extra time if you need it for particularly complex applications. You may solicit more institutional funders than will fit in this chart. If so, just note the largest ones. Many funders have rolling deadlines or multiple submission opportunities each year. Reduce stress by spreading grantswriting evenly across the year. Schedule your biggest funders with set deadlines first; then fit funders with multiple or rolling deadlines in the gaps between. You may find yourself applying to and receiving grants from a funder at the same time each year. If so, you may want to stick to that schedule so that you don't fall out of the grantmaking cycle. Acknowledge funders' long lead times. The proposal you submit in April may be awarded in June to fund a program that starts in September of your next fiscal year.

Your nonprofit may back up the one-page plan with more detail, a budget for departmental income and expense, for example, or strategies for acquiring new donors or increasing sponsorship. The one-page plan is designed for board, not staff. It's a high-level view to help your team work together and stay on track. And for nonprofits who lack a plan, it's an easy way to get started.

GET GRANTS

> "Because everyone who keeps asking will receive, and the person who keeps searching will find, and the person who keeps knocking will have the door opened."
>
> —Matthew 7:8, International Standard Version Bible

Fundraising from corporations, foundations, and government agencies follows the same five steps as fundraising from individuals, with one advantage.

Individuals don't come with fundraising instructions. Institutional funders do.

Most foundations, corporations, and government agencies publish their guidelines and preferences, the kinds of projects they'll fund, and those they won't. They have no interest in being flooded with hundreds of applications that don't fit their guidelines. Nor do they want nonprofits to waste time developing proposals that won't be funded. Allow me to summarize the ways fundraising from institutions differs from asking individuals.

Thanking is also called acknowledgment or recognition when dealing with institutional funders. While it's good manners to thank individual donors, recognizing institutional funders may be required and the manner of acknowledgment prescribed. For example, most companies want to review and approve any use of their name or logo before you publish, post, or include them in a press release. Government funders may require you to acknowledge grants in very specific ways, such as by posting a sign by the facility you're building with public dollars. Foundations may not require you to recognize their support, but if you do so, they may specify the wording you use.

Institutional funders send award letters that may specify what their grant can be used for, as well as recognition and reporting requirements. By cashing the funder's check, your nonprofit agrees to the terms of the grant. Some funders are even more explicit, requiring the executive director to sign a legally binding letter of acceptance. Whatever the conditions, the development office should keep such correspondence on file and ensure your nonprofit fulfills its terms.

Engaging, like thanking, may be mandated by institutional funders. It's only fair that you tell them what you did with their last grant before asking for another one. Your nonprofit should put systems in place to collect reporting data at the beginning of the grant period, not at the end. Let's say you got your math camp funded by claiming participants would retain their school-year lessons at twice the rate of noncamp peers. Your nonprofit should establish a control group, tracking and comparing their math retention with that of your campers. This benchmarking should take place at the beginning and at the end of the summer. Otherwise, how will you document your effectiveness in your follow-up report?

Grants must be used for the purpose described in your proposal. As a board member, you'll want to know which funds are restricted and which are unrestricted. If your plans change or you are unable to fulfill the terms of a restricted grant, you should speak to the funder immediately. If your reasons are good, they may allow you more time to complete the proposed project or permit you to secure additional funds from other sources. In rare instances, they may allow you redirect the funds for another purpose, but that is up to them, not you. You should ask first and get approval for changes in writing. Grantmaking is a serious business. If you can't fulfill your end of the deal, funders are within their rights to take their money back.

Researching foundations is relatively easy. You can view their 990 tax returns through free registration on GuideStar (www.guidestar.org). Their 990 contains contact information, how much they donated, and the amounts awarded to each recipient. The 990 also lists the foundation's board of directors, which is handy if you happen to know someone. The 990 reflects information that is at least a year or two old. Foundations can change their guidelines, deadlines, and focus, so check their websites for the most current data.

If you don't know who to ask, the Foundation Directory Online (FDO) is an excellent resource (https://fconline.foundationcenter.org), though pricey for smaller nonprofits. The FDO allows you to search by interest area (e.g., early childhood education), region (e.g., giving by state), types of funding (e.g., capital campaigns), and many other criteria. The FDO is a service provided by the Foundation Center, which has hubs offering free resources in several major U.S. cities, and more than 400 network centers in libraries around the world. The easiest research may be checking the donor lists of charities like your own. Foundations supporting your peers may be good prospects for you, especially if your programs complement, but don't replicate, the services of related nonprofits.

Researching corporations is a bit trickier than researching foundations. If they've established a corporate foundation, you check their 990. Unlike corporate foundations, corporate giving programs aren't required to say who they fund, how much they give, or why. The company's website is your best source of up-to-date info. Look under Corporate Social Responsibility, Community Relations, Corporate Philanthropy, or in their annual report. If you're active on LinkedIn, type in the company name to see if you're connected to any employees. If the company matches employee gifts, check your database. You may find that some of your donors work for that company. Employee donors care about you and can provide useful information. Most are happy to advise you and doing so costs them nothing.

Corporations exist to make money for their shareholders, not to give it away. Strategic companies align giving with their company's mission and/or to reach target markets. For example, an insurance company might support bicycle safety or diabetes testing. A bank might underwrite financial literacy programs. Both might sponsor museum openings to gain access to their target markets of influential CEOs and wealthy individuals. As with foundations, check lists of corporate donors supporting nonprofits with missions or programs akin to yours.

Researching government agencies. At this writing, many U.S. agencies have cut back on grantmaking, but the government may still represent a significant source of funding for your nonprofit. Ask your legislators and agency administrators to help you find funding. It's part of their job to serve constituents, and it's a fast way to identify appropriate resources. Cultivate these friends in high places. Don't be put off if legislators send staff in their place. The director of urban affairs, for example, or the staffer who guides them on the environment may know more about issue-related funding than their bosses ever will.

If you're in the United States, you can start your online research at https:// Grants.Gov. Relevant agencies at the federal, state, and local level all post funding opportunities on their websites. For example, if I wanted money to help juvenile offenders, I'd check the U.S. Department of Justice, Office of Juvenile Justice, and Delinquency Prevention websites. Since I live in Philadelphia, I'd review grants posted on the Pennsylvania Commission on Crime and Delinquency website and on Philadelphia's Office of Juvenile Justice and Department of Human Services websites.

Cultivating foundations and corporations. We used to say, "Work for a foundation and you'll never pay for lunch nor know who your friends are." Meaning everyone will wine and dine you to get funded.

Times have changed.

Foundation officers may scrupulously avoid taking favors from potential grantees or even discussing their work with you in social situations. Some welcome phone calls, others forbid them. Some start the funding process with a simple letter of inquiry (LOI) while others require you to submit a full proposal to begin the conversation. Many will conduct site visits before funding your nonprofit. Do your homework to learn their preferences before you pick up the phone or shoot off an email.

Think of corporations and foundations as investors. They conduct due diligence to get to know you before funding your nonprofit. Put executives from current and potential funders on your VIP list so that they're automatically invited to programs and events. As with individuals, assign a relationship carrier, someone they know or who'll get to know them. This person should call to follow up on invitations. ("Rich and I are going to the kayaking race this weekend. Will you be joining us?") It's nice if they can attend, but even if they decline, they'll know you're thinking of them. These non-asking contacts are the building blocks of funder relationships, and remember, program officers are people, too, usually very good people. I remember one foundation director who was so moved by our children's choir that she made a generous personal donation in addition to the grant her foundation awarded.

Corporate Cinderella. I once saw a cartoon that neatly captured the role of a director of corporate giving. It showed a woman outside her office as the fairy godmother, using her magic want to grant the wishes of grateful nonprofits. Inside, on the other side of the door, she was dressed as Cinderella, scrubbing the office floors.

Let's face it, giving money *away* doesn't put you on the fast track for promotion to CEO. The top corporate jobs go to executives who bring money *in*. Corporate-giving officers have internal audiences to satisfy. Helping them do so can strengthen your relationship with them.

Imagine your nonprofit has ten volunteers who work for RST Corporation, and all ten endorse your request for funding. Assuming your proposal is comparable to those submitted by peer nonprofits, the giving officer will fund your request over one that lacks RST employee support. In doing so, she's satisfied ten internal colleagues and reinforced an existing relationship between her company and your nonprofit. Matching gifts are often treated as employee benefits and managed through human resources. Get to know RST's human resources director, and he or she may guide an RST executive to serve on your board. Similarly, if RST's marketing director wants to reach suburban moms, you might propose a Mother's Day sponsorship opportunity. Have unsold tickets to your play? Offer an employee discount on their in-house bulletin board. It may fill those seats and connect even more employees to your theater.

Cultivating government funders. You can help cultivate relationships with municipal, state, and federal representatives, as well as with relevant agency administrators. Host a legislative breakfast. Invite representatives to events. Give them roles in facility or exhibit openings. Politicians want to be with voters and to affiliate themselves with worthy causes like yours.

Asking. Nonprofit staff usually solicit corporations, foundations, and government agencies, developing proposals and submitting reports. If you happen to know the trustee of a foundation, a corporate executive, or government leader, introduce them to your nonprofit. Such meetings allow your staff to ask questions, possibly learning what's needed to craft a winning proposal. Or, you may lend discipline-specific knowledge. For example, if you're on a soup kitchen board because you're a nutritionist or on a historical society board because you're a scholar, your credentials may strengthen the proposal, even if you're not listed as a principal investigator (PI).

MAKE TECHNOLOGY YOUR FRIEND

"Nobody's going to fix the world for us, but working together, making use of technological innovations and human communities, we might just fix it ourselves."

—Jamais Cascio

I prefer simple, dependable, user-friendly fundraising software over fancy databases with lots of bells and whistles that no one knows how to use.

As a board member, you don't need to be a techno-wiz. I'd like to suggest four key concepts that may help you lead more effectively: (1) love your database, (2) make online giving easy, (3) don't confuse social media with fundraising, and (4) use crowdfunding to build your base.

Love Your Database *Underdeveloped: A National Study of Challenges Facing Nonprofit Fundraising* found *21 percent of nonprofits have no fundraising database at all.*[6] Even if your nonprofit has one, you may lack the staff to manage it or the tech support to keep it functioning. Don't assume your nonprofit's e-blast service is tied to your donor base or that it can send emails to donors based on their giving history. It probably can't.

Do you think the gent who asked Mrs. T. to give last year is flagged as her solicitor? He may not be. Are the notes from yesterday's rating session entered in your database? Highly unlikely. Maybe in a month, but not today.

Staff at smaller nonprofits want top-notch data, but they're stretched thin, with little time to document what they've done or to build the infrastructure needed to grow. Ask what your nonprofit's constituent management software (CRM) can and cannot do. Discover what frustrates staff. Ask them to generate a one-page call sheet with your name, contact info, giving history, and interactions with your nonprofit. If they can't do it, you may want to invest in infrastructure. You need functional fundraising software to manage the five-step asking process. If necessary, raise funds to get your system up to speed. Your database is the heart, soul, brain, and institutional memory of your nonprofit's funding.

Note: If your nonprofit has a superbly functioning, fully populated database, manned by well-trained staff, congratulations! Just don't assume this is true until you investigate.

Make Online Giving Easy Online giving continues to grow, according to the latest Charitable Giving Report produced by the Blackbaud Institute for Philanthropic Research.[7] Today, more than 7 percent of all charitable gifts donated in the United States, Canada, and the United Kingdom are made online, and of those, 17 percent are made on mobile devices. Try making a small donation to your nonprofit from your smartphone or tablet. If it's hard to find, see, or navigate, you could be losing donors. Do what you must to make mobile giving effortless.

Don't Confuse Social Media with Fundraising Use social media to broadcast your message, expand your following, and position your nonprofit at the heart of relevant conversations, but don't confuse it with fundraising. Consider the return on investment. How much will ten hours of grants writing earn versus ten hours of social media posting? Don't spend precious resources on social media if it keeps staff from work that will result in needed funding.

Use Crowdfunding to Build Your Base   Crowdfunding can be a great acquisition or clean-up campaign, but you'll likely raise more money from one visit to a major donor. Imagine your funding streams as a diversified investment portfolio. The bulk of your revenue is generated from steady sources, your annual fund, and repeat grants. You must constantly replenish lost donors, and crowdfunding can be an exciting way to bring new donors into the fold. But the return on investment can be low. Crowdfunding represents the high-risk, growth portion of your portfolio. You wouldn't put all your money there, but it may yield significant returns over time and can balance more conservative investments.

You are a board member, not a development professional. Equipped with a one-page development plan, an understanding of institutional funders, and dependable technology, you can lead your committee to success.

ACTIVITY: One-Page Development Plan

Create your own one-page development plan using the template in the Fundraiser's Toolkit at the end of this book.

GET YOUR CAPE ON

> "Step into the fire of self-discovery. This fire will not burn you, it will only burn what you are not."
>
> —Mooji

Who are you? What do you want? And why?

At the beginning of this book, I asked you to write your personal mission statement, documenting, perhaps for the first time, what's important to you, what you value, who you admire, and what you'd like to achieve.

In other words, I asked who you are, what you want, and why.

If you didn't complete your mission statement then, do it now, using the Franklin Covey template (https://msb.franklincovey.com). If you wrote it earlier, pull it out, because serving on a board isn't just a duty. It's a chance to advance your personal goals and fulfill your heart's desire. Through it, you can engage your passion, enjoy the comradery of like-minded souls, grow your skills, connect deeply, and make a difference, as these nonprofit heroes did.

Passion

I know a financier who loved the violin but never made time to play until he joined the board of a music school. I know a litigator who acted in college. Despite a grueling work schedule, serving on a theater board energized him.

Comradery

We can't always choose our office mates, but we can choose our board. It's a pleasure to work with like-minded souls to advance a cause you care about.

I know a birder whose avian interests bored his wife, but who found an enthusiastic audience at the Audubon Society. I know an executive who feels serving on the Urban League board keeps him connected to his roots. It allows him to help build economic independence for black families, a cause he cares about deeply. If you are the company you keep, you may find ennobling friends on a nonprofit board.

Growth

An executive once told me that leading a nonprofit prepared him for his first presentation to a corporate board. He knew the rules of the game, did well, and eventually became CEO of the company that employs him.

You get to know your fellow board members by how they respond to pressure, their sense of humor, creativity, and determination. I know executives who were hired by fellow board members, and who, in turn, hired colleagues they'd met through board service. A sales executive joined his nonprofit's HR committee, chaired by one of the region's experts. The knowledge he gained served him well when he became a manager.

Connections

It's easy to be consumed by work and family. Volunteering gets you out of your box and into the community. If you're thoughtful about it, you can choose a board that provides quality time with your loved ones. For example, if you have children, you might join the board of a bicycling group. You will have to attend your nonprofit's events anyway, so why not bring your kids and share your love of the open road with them?

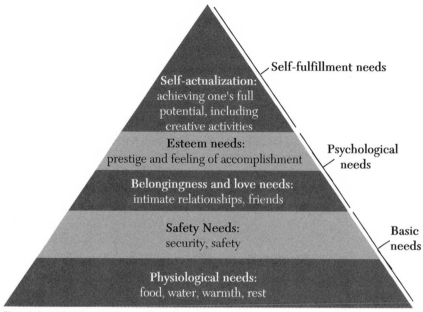

Fig. 4.1. Maslow's hierarchy of needs
©VMJA 2018

Impact

You may know Maslow's hierarchy of human needs, which states that our most basic needs are physiological, including food, water, warmth, and rest (see figure 4.1). After those are satisfied, we require safety in the form of security and shelter. Next, we need to belong to a community to have relationships with friends and family. Once our physical and social needs are met, we need the self-esteem we derive from achievement, mastery, and the recognition of others. Our highest need is self-actualization, which Maslow describes as pursuit of your talents, creativity, and personal fulfillment. I call it impact. For who among us wants to end our life having changed nothing? Having helped no one? Having contributed nothing to the glorious tapestry of human existence? We want to make our mark, and we can do that through nonprofit leadership.

Here are a few examples. Inner-city kids will receive 5,000 hours of vocal training thanks to one board member I admire. A new play was mounted because another board member raised the money to commission it. I know a mom whose neighborhood is safer thanks to her vigilant town watch leadership.

Tap your deepest passion, find comrades, grow, connect, and make an impact through board service. Standing strong in who you are, what you want, and knowing why, you can ask for and get gifts that will change the world.

Start with the Easy Steps

"Assign a hard job to a lazy man; he's sure to find an easy way to do it."

—Business saying

There's a lingering Puritan streak in American culture. We regard the hard-working laborer with approval, but are suspicious of his clever, lazy neighbor, who can take it easy because he figured out how he could do the job in half the time. We can't afford to fundraise the hard way and we certainly can't afford our current situation, with thousands of board members frozen to inactivity because they can't, won't, or don't know how to fundraise.

Start with a step, any step. It will help your nonprofit more than sitting on the sidelines.

If you like to thank, have at it. Your nonprofit probably has major donors who've not been thanked by a board member in years. Are you shy, but fond of research? Your nonprofit may welcome your help, and you may find it's fun, like a scavenger hunt for donors. Or, you may bring a fresh perspective to routine tasks. Like the lazy man, you may see a more efficient way of working. If so, speak up!

Do One Step Superbly

"Simplicity is the ultimate sophistication."

—William Gaddis

It's easy to get overwhelmed by fundraising. There's so much to do and so little time to do it. As a volunteer, you want to help as much as possible. You may want to run all the events, write reports, research donors, and visit 100 funders and donors. But few of us can manage that. Start easy and focus on the tasks you do best. Your asking personality profile in chapter 3 will suggest steps you'll prefer and at which you'll likely excel. Pick one, set yourself a goal, and get good at it.

Let's say you love research. If you spend your four years on the board identifying and researching hundreds of prospective donors, you'll make an invaluable contribution to the fundraising effort. As I mentioned earlier, some charities lose half their donors each year. Your efforts to replace them may be critical to your nonprofit's success.

All of us can find natural ways to do each step in the fundraising process, and I hope you will. But if your time is limited, it's better to do one step superbly than to spread yourself too thin or do nothing at all.

What You Can Do, Right Now, for Free, to Help Raise Money

> "Not all of us can do great things. But we can do small things with great love."
>
> —Mother Teresa

Being a nonprofit hero isn't all that hard. You already know the basics. Professional fundraisers use the same steps I've taught you. They ask, thank, engage, then research, cultivate, and ask new prospects all over again. I've flipped the order, but the steps are the same. Know who you are, what you want and why, choose your cause carefully, start easy, and play to your strengths and you'll be ahead of 90 percent of board fundraisers!

Let's review the easy, specific, and free things you can do to raise more money.

1. Create your giving dos and don'ts and keep them in mind when approaching donors.
2. Identify your fears and objections through the *Yeah, but . . .* activity. Learn to honor and address each one until you can turn it into an asset.
3. Build your personal mission statement and align it with a cause that fulfills you.
4. Find your asking personality based on your Myers-Briggs type. Learn how to use it to play to your strengths in each step of the asking process.
5. Assign thankers to create and deepen relationships with donors.
6. Use thank-a-thons and thank-you note writing parties to spark contagious gratitude.
7. Recognize and encourage monthly and cumulative giving.
8. Survey donors to find what volunteer activities they'd find most fulfilling. Matching person to task if/as possible.

9. List your nonprofit's engagement activities; brainstorm more creative ones if needed.
10. Start meetings with one vivid experience or memorable impact story.
11. Create your own impact story journal and add to it regularly.
12. Assign an optimistic reader to generate a constant flow of new prospects.
13. As a board, review lists of new members, donors, and visitors . . . often.
14. Use LinkedIn to connect with members of your nonprofit's board and staff.
15. Get and read prospects' bios to identify possible connections.
16. In addition to dollar goals, set site visit goals that offer memorable experiences.
17. Station "farewellers" to speak to people as they leave your events.
18. Use the Cultivation Activity chart to match donors and friends to the right activities.
19. Give first, generously and thoughtfully, before asking others to donate.
20. Have board members ask three donors before they solicit one nondonor.
21. Develop two to three funding ideas for each major donor you visit.
22. Keep your sense of humor and stay open to the possibility of a positive outcome, even from a difficult conversation.
23. Listen to your donor, waiting at least three beats after they've finished before you speak.
24. Do the "elevate your speech" activity to get comfortable talking about your cause.
25. Use chapter 3's quick tips chart to remember who, how, and what you should ask for.
26. Get happy, using the steps in your happiness journal.
27. Draft your previsit email and script for calling to schedule appointments.
28. Got happy, using the steps in your happines journal.
29. Review or create a job description for members of your development committee.
30. Request or create a one-page development plan.

Each of these tasks is easy. Use the ones you find useful and skip the rest. I promise, there won't be a test. But the more of these you do, the easier your fundraising will become.

Heroic Attributes

"We do not see things as they are. We see them as we are."

—The Talmud

We define ourselves, in large part, by what we do and how others see us. We want to be perceived as good, gracious, fun, supportive, smart, talented, attractive, accomplished, and lovable. We embrace things that feed our positive self-image. "If I wear this suit, I'll look distinguished." "I'm posting my award on social media!" "Look at me making her Halloween costume from scratch. I'm such a good mom." And we avoid things that diminish our sense of self. "If I ask her to pick up my kids again, she'll think I'm a leech." "I'm annoying him with these constant rewrites." "This dress makes me look fat."

So, how do you feel about fundraising?

You've seen how *attentive, confident,* and *connected* board fundraisers can be. You may have been encouraged to see it required *creativity.* Maybe you liked the idea of channeling your natural *curiosity, empathy, sincerity,* and *observational* skills to raise funds. You probably hadn't thought of *gratitude* as part of fundraising or considered how you might use it to *empower* others. By now you know development involves using your *vibrant* love of life and *optimistic* view of the future to *inspire* others. Like Arthur's knights of the round table, you are an *honorable* leader who can *transform* people's lives, making a long-lasting, positive *impact.*

Curiosity, empathy, creativity, honor, gratitude, and inspiration: each of these is a part of fundraising and each is a positive attribute I hope you can embrace.

We need you!

Go Out and Change the World!

"We never know how high we are till we are called to rise; and then, if we are true to plan, our statures touch the skies."

—Emily Dickinson

We began by learning what we hate about asking and conclude with fundraising's ability to call forth the best in you, how it can help you achieve your dreams, satisfy your desires, and fulfill your personal mission in life.

I've trained more than a thousand volunteer and professional leaders in the nonprofit hero method and it gets results. Studies show 100 percent of the boards that I train are more willing to fundraise and confident doing so. One group almost doubled the number of board members willing to ask for major gifts. Another nonprofit doubled its base of donors in under six months.

If they can do it, so can you.

Know what you want, start with easy steps, play to your strengths, and ask.

Now, get your cape on!

THE FUNDRAISER'S TOOLKIT

TOOLS YOU CAN USE

I'm an inveterate collector. When I come across samples I like or useful templates, I snag them and stick them in my "Tools" folder. When I spend days developing new systems or budgets, I file them, knowing they'll provide solid launching pads for future projects. When I begin drafting a new case statement, I review old ones for structure and inspiration. Sometimes, looking at samples reminds me of what I don't like, what I want to add or change. Throughout this book, I refer to the samples, templates, and resources below. I hope they save you time and help you ask as the nonprofit hero that you are.

1. Sample giving dos and don'ts demonstrate how you can complete the first exercise in chapter one of this book.
2. Sample "*Yeah, buts . . .*" lists some common board asking fears.
3. Sample thank-you note provides a framework for writing your own.
4. Sample cultivation activities chart shows you how you might use the chart for your own nonprofit.
5. Sample email requesting a visit paves the way for your scheduling call.
6. Sample phone script shows you how to follow up on your email.
7. Template asking script follows the outline described in this book.
8. Sample development committee job description is followed by links to additional resources.
9. Template for a development plan you can use to draft your own one-page plan in about an hour.

10. Online resources include many helpful links, including the Valerie M. Jones Associates website where we'll add resources for years after you buy this book.

1. SAMPLE: GIVING DOS AND DON'TS

Sample Do Gift

Gift: "We endowed a Greenland College engineering scholarship."

What made that gift satisfying? "We were so grateful for our son Arthur's transformation. He was an insecure, confused, and reclusive freshman. When he graduated, he was self-assured, had found his life's passion, and made friends. You might think it would've happened anywhere; we don't. Greenland created a unique culture of learning, attracted the kinds of students Arthur clicked with, and his professors took a real interest. We wanted to say thank you in a meaningful way and give others the same opportunity our son had. We love hearing from the students, all different and yet all catching fire somehow."

Sample Don't Gifts

Gift: "I made a gift to the United Way."

Why was it disappointing? "I was strong-armed into giving at work. They wouldn't even let me direct my gift to a charity I cared about. I gave, and I'll have to do it again, but I resent it."

Gift: "I made a gift to the local animal shelter."

Why was it disappointing? "My best friend, Samantha, is active with this organization, but I got a generic appeal letter, and, when I gave, received an equally generic thank-you. I contributed because I knew she was involved, but if she doesn't care whether I give or not, why should I? Plus, I suspect there must be something wrong with this place, or she would've asked me herself, wouldn't she? I won't give in the future."

2. SAMPLE: YEAH, BUTS . . .

Yeah, I'd like to ask for a $1,000 gift, *but* . . .

- They'll probably say no.
- I'll be rejected.
- It'll ruin our friendship.
- They'll think I only want them for their money.

- It's too much.
- I don't know who to ask.
- I don't know what to ask for.
- I don't know what to say.
- I don't know them well enough/at all.
- I don't know how much to ask for . . . maybe they could give more.
- I'm afraid they'll ask me questions that I can't answer.
- It's a bad time for them (divorce, they're putting kids through college, unemployed, etc.).
- I'm nervous/scared.
- I need privacy.
- I don't know their relationship to us. Maybe they've just given or told us not to ask.
- I'm not the best person. Someone else probably knows them better.
- If I ask them, they'll ask me to give $1,000 to their nonprofit, and I can't/don't want to.

3. SAMPLE: THANK-YOU NOTE

Dear Ava,

Thank you so much for your gift of $100 to the Spirit Center.

Visiting the center last week I was grateful to you for making its serenity, outreach, and spiritual guidance possible. The land, with its stubbly fields, sleeping woodlands, and air sharp with frost and wood smoke, soothed me as it does all who find their way there.

Last summer, our farm manager, Mariyah, helped refugees set up a Halal community garden. The children swarmed around her, carrying dirt and watering their own little muddy patches. A five-year-old clung to her mother and wouldn't participate until Mariyah put a bean in her hand. Twenty minutes later, this shell-shocked child had released her mother and was solemnly planting her seed with the other children. Amazing.

I'll be driving up for the winter retreat on February 7. Can you join us? I'd love to introduce you to our executive director, Serena, and could give you a lift. Just let me know.

Once again, thanks so much for your generosity, for supporting our peacemaking, and for helping feed and shelter refugee families who have suffered so much.

Sincerely yours,

Susan Callaghan

Board member

P.S.: If you can't come in February, we're having an "extended family" Lailat Al Miraj banquet May 13, featuring early produce from the center. Kids are welcome, and it's a lot of fun.

4. SAMPLE: CULTIVATION ACTIVITIES CHART FOR BALLET

Table 5.1. Sample Cultivation Activity Chart (Completed) ©VMJA 2018

Cultivation activity	List three people you could invite	Activity date(s)	Is it free or will it cost? How much?	If it costs, do you or does your nonprofit pay?
A. The Nutcracker Sensory-friendly performances	1. Naomi 2. Stephanie 3. Gina	Late Nov.– mid Dec.	$30–$100/ person	Attendees pay.
B. Dance studio visit	1. Brenda and Don 2. Blake 3. Liza	Groups by request	Free to visitors	Ballet covers cost.
C. Outreach Project* Annual performance	1. Brianna 2. Julia 3. Melissa	End of school year	Free? Not sure, must check.	Not sure, must check.

Note: The ballet offers free classes to introduce urban schoolchildren to ballet. Each year, students from several schools are chosen to perform on stage with professionals.

5. SAMPLE: EMAIL REQUESTING A VISIT

Header: Time with Chris Bernier re: Headland Lighthouse Plans for 200th

This is the most important part of your email. It should not read like a generic nonprofit email, nor like a fundraising appeal, nor, for goodness sake, like spam. Personalize it enough so the recipient quickly sees it's from you. Don't assume your return email is enough.

Salutation: "Dear Phyllis." *Address them as you would in person. Check that you spell their name/nickname correctly.*

Intro: "Hi! Hope this finds you and George well. Jann and I are looking forward to seeing you when we open our summer house in Maine next week." *Establish personal connection.*

Purpose: "Can I set a time to take you to the lighthouse the following week? You've been so generous to the Friends of the Headland Lighthouse. I'd like you to experience the new trails for yourself. I'd also like to introduce you to their dynamic founder, Elena Jones. She has some terrific ideas for the lighthouse's 200th anniversary. We want to do this right and would welcome your feedback on our plans, especially since you've so much experience with historic properties." *Tell them you'll call to set a date and describe the project briefly, in just one or two sentences.*

Next step: "I think you come in Friday night. I'll give you a couple days to settle in and call Monday to see when I can take you over in the skiff." *Tell them when you'll call.*

Personal close: "Let me know if there's anything we can pick up for you. Meanwhile, travel safe, and see you next week!"

"Best, Chris." Include contact info in your e-signature to be sure they have it.

6. SAMPLE: PHONE SCRIPT FOR SCHEDULING A VISIT

Opening: "Hi, Phyllis. Welcome back to Maine. How was your trip? Everything okay with the house?" *Listen. Respond.*

Schedule: "I promised to call so we could make a date to take you and George over to Headland Lighthouse next week. There's lots going on and I want to introduce you to Elena Jones. She'll be there Tuesday morning from 10:30 to noon and Thursday afternoon from 3 p.m. to sunset. Which would work better for you guys?" *Listen. Confirm.*

"Great! I'll let Elena know we'll join her at 4 p.m. next Thursday at the lighthouse. I'll pick you up at the dock at 3:30 p.m. See you then."

Get off!

7. TEMPLATE: ASKING SCRIPT

Opening

Remind them why you're meeting.
Confirm how much time you have.
Catch up personally/socially. (Briefly)
Share your motivation/involvement. (Briefly)

Transition Question: Such as, "So, what sparked your interest in XYZ Nonprofit?"

Discuss Your Nonprofit

Listen to your donor/prospect's response.
Note any comments that relate to your nonprofit's needs.
Summarize the situation.

1. First point: Listen to their response.
2. Second point: Listen to their response.
3. Third point: Listen to their response.

Transition Question: Such as, "Do you have any questions about XYZ Nonprofit?"
Listen.

Ask for the Gift

Transition Questions:

Donors: Thank them for past support, remind them of their impact, and invite them to join you by considering a gift of . . . or by considering a gift in the range of . . .
Prospects: Remind them of the impact they can make and invite them to join you by considering a gift of . . . or by considering a gift in the range of . . .

Listen to their response.

Their Decision

Yes Listen. Thank them. Have them fill out the pledge form, if appropriate.

Confirm next steps.

Maybe Listen. Try to learn what's needed to make a decision and help them do so if possible.

If still unresolved, suggest possible next steps and a time when you will follow up.

No Listen to hear why. Let them talk. If they want to help your cause, offer ways to overcome perceived barriers, such as paying over time. If it's a clear and definite no, tell them you're always trying to improve, and ask them if there's anything you or your nonprofit could do to win their support. If they don't want to give but do want to help, suggest volunteering opportunities. Thank them for their honesty and time; reiterate next steps, if any.

Transition Question: Whatever their decision, repeat it back to them and ask, "Have I understood you correctly?"

Listen. Hopefully, you're on the same page. If not, get clarity.

Next Steps, Closure, and Follow-Up

Transition Question: "Is there anything more I can do or answer for you before I go?"

Listen.

If they raise any new issues, address them if you can.

Confirm next steps.

Thank them again for their consideration and support, if appropriate.

Circle back to your personal connection to close out the visit, such as, "Tell Barbara I'm sorry I missed her," or, "Let us know if you can come to the beach house next week."

Say goodbye.

Postvisit

If you got a gift or pledge, give it to your nonprofit ASAP.

Write your donor a thank-you email or note summarizing the meeting.

Copy or resend that to your development office.

Complete any promised tasks, such as sending info, tickets, and so forth.

8. SAMPLE: DEVELOPMENT COMMITTEE JOB DESCRIPTION—XYZ BOARD OF DIRECTORS

Mission

XYZ Nonprofit's development committee exists to secure contributed and fee-for-service revenue in support of XYZ's programs and activities.

Goal

Lead the board in securing $_____ each year and introducing __ new donors to our cause.

Responsibilities

- To get to know XYZ, including, but not limited to, attending _____, _____, and _____.
- To help identify and recruit volunteers for the development committee and the board.
- To attend regularly scheduled committee meetings.
- To thank, engage, identify/research, cultivate, and participate in the fundraising process on behalf of XYZ.
- To represent XYZ, as needed, at press and other events.
- To make a "stretch gift" to XYZ annually. A "stretch gift" is defined as giving more than you would give were you not on the board, in a way that sets a positive example.
- To personally bring __ individuals or more to visit XYZ and/or experience its programs.
- To personally participate in the process of securing $___ or more in gifts annually.

Term

Committee members serve for a two-year, renewable term while on the board.

More sample board job descriptions can be found on the following sites:

- www.bridgespan.org/insights/library/hiring/nonprofit-job-description-toolkit/board-job-descriptions
- www.compasspoint.org/board-cafe/sample-job-descriptions-board-officers
- www.nonprofitadvancement.org/category/resource-type/samples-templates
- https://boardsource.org/resources/board-member-job-description/

9. TEMPLATE: ONE-PAGE DEVELOPMENT PLAN

Table 5.2. Template One-Page Development Plan (Blank) ©VMJA 2018

Campaigns	July	August	September	October	November	December	January	February	March	April	May	June
Board campaign ____ Chair $ ____ Goal												
Major gifts $1,000+ donors ____ Chair $ ____ Goal												
Annual fund <$1,000 donors & prospects ____ Chair $ ____ Goal												
Grants— Corporate, foundation & government (staff leads) $ ____ Goal												
Corporate sponsorship ____ Chair $ ____ Goal												
Gala ____ & ____ Chair $ ____ Goal												
Proposed 5K run ____ Chair $ ____ Goal												

10: ONLINE RESOURCES

Below are links to some of the most useful online resources mentioned in this book, as well as some additional favorites. It's by no means comprehensive, and I hope you'll add your own. I'll continue to share my favorites on my website, www.vmja.com, my blog, and on social media, including on Twitter @ValJFundraising, on LinkedIn at www.linkedin.com/in/valeriem jonescfre/, and as ValJonesFundraising on Facebook.

Change the "You" Who Shows Up

- Shawn Achor, *The Happiness Advantage,* www.GoodThinkInc.com, or check out his TED Talk on www.ted.com.
- Create your personal mission statement at http://msbfranklincovey .com (free).

Find a Nonprofit That's Right for You

These are free, though some offer additional help through membership, paid subscription, and/or books and other materials.

- www.bridgespan.org
- www.boardnetusa.org
- www.volunteermatch.org
- www.linkedin.com
- www.chamberofcommerce.com (Find your local chamber; then see if they have a leadership or training program for those who want to serve on nonprofit boards.)

Find Your Asking Personality

Find your type so you can discover your asking personality profile:

- www.mbtionline.com (paid)
- www.humanmetrics.com (free)
- www.16personalities.com (free)

Set Your Goals and Lead Your Team

- https://home.idonethis.com (paid)
- www.stickk.com (paid)

- http://mycommittee.com (paid)
- www.boardeffect.com (paid)

Find and research potential funders:

- www.guidestar.com (free)
- https://fconline.foundationcenter.org (paid)
- https://grants.gov (free)
- www.nozasearch.com (paid, with some parts free)

Free for foundation info, must pay subscription to access gifts from corporate and individuals.

Helpful all-purpose sites and journals:

- http://www.blueavocado.org/category/topic/board-cafe (free) Funny, smart, short enough to read over a cup of coffee. My favorite e-news for board members and nonprofit executives.
- www.networkforgood.com (free also, offers good, low-cost webinars)
- https://boardsource.org (free to visit)
- https://charitychannel.com (free)
- https://nonprofitlearninglab.org (low-cost paid classes)
- www.charitynavigator.com (free)
- www.chronicleofphilanthropy.com (free daily e-blasts requires paid subscription to access all content)

Raise a little money and awareness with services that generate gifts for your nonprofit:

- www.goodsearch.com: Generates pennies when you use its search engine and more if you buy products via Good Shop. You must log in to your profile before searching.
- smile.amazon.com: Donates a portion of your Amazon purchases to your designated nonprofit. You must remember to log in to Smile before buying.
- contribute.surveymonkey.com/sign-up/profile: Some surveys will donate to your nonprofit, sometimes several dollars for each survey completed.

There are many similar services that generate small donations when your constituents use them to make purchases or browse the internet. These are the three I have personally audited for my own clients and found the funds they claim to generate were in fact paid out.

NOTES

CHAPTER 1

1. Network for Good. *The Nonprofit Marketing Blog*, October 6, 2015. https://www.networkforgood.com/nonprofitblog/how-to-get-non-profit-donations/.

CHAPTER 2

1. Levis, Bill—The Urban Institute; Ben Miller—DonorTrends; and Cathy Williams—Association of Fundraising Professionals. *2016 Fundraising Effectiveness Survey Report*, March 19, 2016. http://www.afpnet.org/files/ContentDocuments/FEP2016FinalReport.pdf.
2. Dilenschneider, Colleen. "Know Your Own Bone." https://www.colleendilen.com/2016/04/20/why-donors-stop-giving-money-to-cultural-organizations-data/.
3. Bell, Jeanne, and Marla Cornelius. *Underdeveloped: A National Study of Challenges Facing Nonprofit Fundraising*. 2013. http://www.giarts.org/sites/default/files/Underdeveloped-National-Study-of-Challenges-Facing-Nonprofit-Fundraising.pdf.

CHAPTER 3

1. The Myers & Briggs Foundation. http://www.myersbriggs.org/my-mbti-personality-type/mbti-basics/the-16-mbti-types.htm?bhcp=1.

2. The Myers & Briggs Foundation." http://www.myersbriggs.org/my-mbti-personality-type/my-mbti-results/how-frequent-is-my-type.htm.

3. Fogal, Robert E. "Just Your Type—or Not!" Fall 2015. https://www.afpnet.org/files/Conference/50-5320Research%20Fall%202015.pdf.

4. The Myers & Briggs Foundation. http://www.myersbriggs.org/my-mbti-personality-type/mbti-basics/the-16-mbti-types.htm?bhcp=1.

5. The Myers & Briggs Foundation. http://www.myersbriggs.org/my-mbti-personality-type/my-mbti-results/how-frequent-is-my-type.htm.

6. Fogal, Robert E. "Just Your Type—or Not!" Fall 2015. https://www.afpnet.org/files/Conference/50-53%20Research%20Fall%202015.pdf.

7. The Myers & Briggs Foundation. http://www.myersbriggs.org/my-mbti-personality-type/mbti-basics/the-16-mbti-types.htm?bhcp=1.

8. The Myers & Briggs Foundation. http://www.myersbriggs.org/my-mbti-personality-type/my-mbti-results/how-frequent-is-my-type.htm.

9. Fogal, Robert E. "Just Your Type—or Not!" Fall 2015. https://www.afpnet.org/files/Conference/50-53%20Research%20Fall%202015.pdf.

10. The Myers & Briggs Foundation. http://www.myersbriggs.org/my-mbti-personality-type/mbti-basics/the-16-mbti-types.htm?bhcp=1.

11. The Myers & Briggs Foundation. http://www.myersbriggs.org/my-mbti-personality-type/my-mbti-results/how-frequent-is-my-type.htm.

12. Fogal, Robert E. "Just Your Type—or Not!" Fall 2015. https://www.afpnet.org/files/Conference/50-53%20Research%20Fall%202015.pdf.

13. The Myers & Briggs Foundation. http://www.myersbriggs.org/my-mbti-personality-type/mbti-basics/the-16-mbti-types.htm?bhcp=1.

14. The Myers & Briggs Foundation. http://www.myersbriggs.org/my-mbti-personality-type/my-mbti-results/how-frequent-is-my-type.htm.

15. Fogal, Robert E. "Just Your Type—or Not!" Fall 2015. https://www.afpnet.org/files/Conference/50-53%20Research%20Fall%202015.pdf.

16. The Myers & Briggs Foundation. http://www.myersbriggs.org/my-mbti-personality-type/mbti-basics/the-16-mbti-types.htm?bhcp=1.

17. The Myers & Briggs Foundation. http://www.myersbriggs.org/my-mbti-personality-type/my-mbti-results/how-frequent-is-my-type.htm.

18. Fogal, Robert E. "Just Your Type—or Not!" Fall 2015. https://www.afpnet.org/files/Conference/50-53 20Research%20Fall%202015.pdf.

19. The Myers & Briggs Foundation. http://www.myersbriggs.org/my-mbti-personality-type/mbti-basics/the-16-mbti-types.htm?bhcp=1.

20. The Myers & Briggs Foundation. http://www.myersbriggs.org/my-mbti-personality-type/my-mbti-results/how-frequent-is-my-type.htm.

21. Fogal, Robert E. "Just Your Type—or Not!" Fall 2015. https://www.afpnet.org/files/Conference/50-53%20Research%20Fall%202015.pdf.

22. The Myers & Briggs Foundation. http://www.myersbriggs.org/my-mbti-personality-type/mbti-basics/the-16-mbti-types.htm?bhcp=1.

23. The Myers & Briggs Foundation. http://www.myersbriggs.org/my-mbti-personality-type/my-mbti-results/how-frequent-is-my-type.htm.

24. Fogal, Robert E. "Just Your Type—or Not!" Fall 2015. https://www.afpnet.org/files/Conference/50-53%20Research%20Fall%202015.pdf.

25. The Myers & Briggs Foundation. http://www.myersbriggs.org/my-mbti-personality-type/mbti-basics/the-16-mbti-types.htm?bhcp=1.

26. "The Myers & Briggs Foundation. http://www.myersbriggs.org/my-mbti-per sonality-type/my-mbti-results/how-frequent-is-my-type.htm.

27. Fogal, Robert E. "Just Your Type—or Not!" Fall 2015. https://www.afpnet.org/files/Conference/50-53%20Research%20Fall%202015.pdf.

28. The Myers & Briggs Foundation. http://www.myersbriggs.org/my-mbti-personality-type/mbti-basics/the-16-mbti-types.htm?bhcp=1.

29. The Myers & Briggs Foundation. http://www.myersbriggs.org/my-mbti-personality-type/my-mbti-results/how-frequent-is-my-type.htm.

30. Fogal, Robert E. "Just Your Type—or Not!" Fall 2015. https://www.afpnet.org/files/Conference/50-53%20Research%20Fall%202015.pdf.

31. The Myers & Briggs Foundation. http://www.myersbriggs.org/my-mbti-personality-type/mbti-basics/the-16-mbti-types.htm?bhcp=1.

32. The Myers & Briggs Foundation. http://www.myersbriggs.org/my-mbti-personality-type/my-mbti-results/how-frequent-is-my-type.htm.

33. Fogal, Robert E. "Just Your Type–or Not!" Fall 2015. https://www.afpnet.org/files/Conference/50-53%20Research%20Fall%202015.pdf.

34. The Myers & Briggs Foundation. http://www.myersbriggs.org/my-mbti-personality-type/mbti-basics/the-16-mbti-types.htm?bhcp=1.

35. The Myers & Briggs Foundation. http://www.myersbriggs.org/my-mbti-personality-type/my-mbti-results/how-frequent-is-my-type.htm.

36. Fogal, Robert E. "Just Your Type–or Not!" Fall 2015. https://www.afpnet.org/files/Conference/50-53%20Research%20Fall%202015.pdf.

37. The Myers & Briggs Foundation. http://www.myersbriggs.org/my-mbti-personality-type/mbti-basics/the-16-mbti-types.htm?bhcp=1.

38. The Myers & Briggs Foundation. http://www.myersbriggs.org/my-mbti-personality-type/my-mbti-results/how-frequent-is-my-type.htm.

39. Fogal, Robert E. "Just Your Type–or Not!" Fall 2015. https://www.afpnet.org/files/Conference/50-53%20Research%20Fall%202015.pdf.

40. The Myers & Briggs Foundation. http://www.myersbriggs.org/my-mbti-personality-type/mbti-basics/the-16-mbti-types.htm?bhcp=1.

41. The Myers & Briggs Foundation. http://www.myersbriggs.org/my-mbti-personality-type/my-mbti-results/how-frequent-is-my-type.htm.

42. Fogal, Robert E. "Just Your Type–or Not!" Fall 2015. https://www.afpnet.org/files/Conference/50-53%20Research%20Fall%202015.pdf.

43. The Myers & Briggs Foundation. http://www.myersbriggs.org/my-mbti-personality-type/mbti-basics/the-16-mbti-types.htm?bhcp=1.

44. The Myers & Briggs Foundation. http://www.myersbriggs.org/my-mbti-personality-type/my-mbti-results/how-frequent-is-my-type.htm.

45. Fogal, Robert E. "Just Your Type—or Not!" Fall 2015. https://www.afpnet.org/files/Conference/50-53%20Research%20Fall%202015.pdf.

46. The Myers & Briggs Foundation. http://www.myersbriggs.org/my-mbti-personality-type/mbti-basics/the-16-mbti-types.htm?bhcp=1.

47. The Myers & Briggs Foundation. http://www.myersbriggs.org/my-mbti-personality-type/my-mbti-results/how-frequent-is-my-type.htm.

48. Fogal, Robert E. "Just Your Type—or Not!" Fall 2015. https://www.afpnet.org/files/Conference/50-53%20Research%20Fall%202015.pdf.

CHAPTER 4

1. Renter, Elizabeth. "What Generosity Does to Your Brain and Life Expectancy," May 1, 2015. https://health.usnews.com/health-news/health-wellness/articles/2015/05/01/what-generosity-does-to-your-brain-and-life-expectancy.

2. Levis, Bill—The Urban Institute; Ben Miller—DonorTrends; and Cathy Williams—Association of Fundraising Professionals. *2016 Fundraising Effectiveness Survey Report*, March 19, 2016. http://www.afpnet.org/files/ContentDocuments/FEP2016FinalReport.pdf.

3. "National Study Sounds Alarm about Nonprofit Fundraising," January 14, 2013. https://www.haasjr.org/resources/national-study-sounds-alarm-about-nonprofit-fundraising.

4. "Goals Research Summary." https://sidsavara.com/wp-content/uploads/2008/09/researchsummary2.pdf.

5. "National Study Sounds Alarm about Nonprofit Fundraising," January 14, 2013. https://www.haasjr.org/resources/national-study-sounds-alarm-about-nonprofit-fundraising.

6. "National Study Sounds Alarm about Nonprofit Fundraising," January 14, 2013. https://www.haasjr.org/resources/national-study-sounds-alarm-about-nonprofit-fundraising.

7. Edited by Shelnutt, Genna. *How Nonprofit Fundraising Performed in 2016*, 2017. https://institute.blackbaud.com/asset/2016-charitable-giving-report/.

INDEX

ABOUT THE AUTHOR

Valerie M. Jones, CFRE, brings her intelligence, determination, and spirit to the world of fund development. Through her boutique consulting firm, Valerie M. Jones Associates (VMJA), she advises clients on board development, major gifts, strategic planning, prospect research, and grantsmanship.

Jones is a born storyteller and attentive listener who admits to being insatiably curious about people. She's raised over $175 million (and counting) for charities that range from internationally recognized colleges and museums to tiny nonprofits known only to a lucky few.

She is a dynamic and sought-after speaker. The Association of Zoos and Aquariums, International Association of Fundraising Professionals, China's New Museum Technologies Conference, and Dress for Success International are just a few of the groups who've benefitted from Jones's engaging appearances.

She delights in coaching and has taught thousands of volunteer and professional fundraisers to ask in ways that are authentic, inspired, smart, and successful. Her service as president, chair, and member of several boards has given her a compassionate understanding of the challenges of volunteer leadership.

Jones earned her B.A. in anthropology and art from Hamilton and Kirkland Colleges, and was a U.S. finalist for the Rhodes Scholarship in the year women were first allowed to compete.